ARTHUR ASHE

BURKE

JACKIE CHAN

AMPLIN

HECTOR ELIZONDO

MILTON GLASER

EARVIN "MAGIC" JOHNSON

EN KING   CHRIS KLUG

JAY LENO

R

PETER LORD

OLIN POWELL

JOHN MCCAIN

MARTIN RICHARDS

HER REEVE

PAC SHAKUR

DANNY VILLANUEVA

THE BOLDNESS OF BOYS

THE BOLDNESS OF BOYS

FAMOUS MEN TALK ABOUT GROWING UP

SUSAN STRONG

**Andrews McMeel
Publishing**

Kansas City

03 04 05 06 07 KP1 10 9 8 7 6 5 4 3 2 1

Library of Congress Cataloging-in-Publication Data
Strong, Susan, Mrs.
   The boldness of boys : famous men talk about growing up / Susan Strong.
      p. cm.
   ISBN 0-7407-3858-5
      1. Teenage boys. 2. Adolescence. 3. Men—Biography. I. Title.

HQ797.S75 2003
305.235—dc21   2003052153

Book design by Lisa Martin

CONTENTS

CONTENTS

THANKS TO THE CREW

The Boldness of Boys is my leap of faith. Encouraged by mothers raising sons, I was propelled to see that boys get their book, too. My deepest gratitude to the extraordinary men who cared enough to share their experiences with this new generation of soon-to-be heroes. It was an honor to read and hear your stories, and I only wish the conversations could have continued.

This book was enhanced by the wisdom and insight of my nephews. They each set examples of how character rules, how competition is healthy, and how being the nice guy wins. By watching them teach others how it's done, I witnessed compassion, courage, and fearless energy. By listening to them burp the alphabet and watching them melt chocolate in their armpits, I saw twisted yet impressive talent. This is for you, Dylan Strong; Pete Pohl; Jeff Lacko; Sam Pohl; Jimmy, John, and Robby Leonis; and Marcello Martinoli. You each make the world a better place and a great deal funnier.

ACKNOWLEDGMENTS

Love to you, Marla Miller, my muse, my mentor, my editor extraordinaire. To my sisters and brothers, Tracy, Amy, Jeff, and Sid, thank you for encouraging me to trust my cape. Thank you Alison Picard and Jean Lucas for believing in book two.

And endless love and appreciation to my dear Bob, Olivia, and Caitlin Pohl. Waking up to the three of you brings me indescribable happiness. Because of you, my dream life is a reality.

READ THIS FIRST!

"Who cares?" said my fifteen-year-old nephew, flipping through *People* magazine. "Why does anyone want to read this stuff?!" He's got a point. We have become a celebrity-obsessed society—delving into the lives of the rich and famous, looking for any similarities, wondering what it would be like to be them.

However, you have more in common with these famous men than you think. Every man in these pages started out just like you. They did the daily grind at school, experienced embarrassing moments, had their own family battles, suffered through heart-wrenching crushes, competed fiercely in sports, and learned how to define themselves through trial and error.

Welcome to *The Boldness of Boys*. Each man in this book will confirm that you are not alone in your journey, that it's going to be okay. Reading about how they handled situations when they were your age just might help you approach your adventure with more courage, more confidence, and more desire to take those necessary risks in order to get what you want.

There are times when the world plays like a video game gone bad, malfunctioning with no way to fix it. What I learned interviewing and reading about the men profiled in the pages of *The Boldness of Boys* is that they all share a common bond: vision. They all found a way to achieve their dreams and live their lives just as they imagined they could. When they needed help, they asked for it. When they saw opportunity, they went for it. When life knocked them down, they dusted themselves off and started over. This book is not about becoming famous; it's about listening to the beat of your own drummer—to that voice inside that's looking out for your best interest.

Did somebody say this was going to be easy? By now, your parents and teachers have said a zillion times that it's never easy. To get what you want requires hard work and practice. I will add only that they're right. *Terminator* and *Titanic* director James Cameron said this: "There are no shortcuts. You're going to work hard. You may look around and see other people who appear to have it easy, but somewhere along the way, they've paid their dues. And for those few who won the lottery or landed the lead in a hit series at the ripe old age of twelve or so, they're going to pay their dues later. Everybody has to. In order to realize your dreams, you have to learn that work ethic."

That's not to say luck doesn't play a role, but more often than not, you need the smarts—you have to trust your instincts and be able to recognize opportunity when it presents itself. Pay attention. Be ready.

Every man in *The Boldness of Boys* has a story to tell and a dream to share. These guys make great company. If you've had a bad day and think you'll never make the varsity team or you just found out that that girl you've had your eye on since third grade is going out with the school jock, join the club. But . . . don't give up. Championship days are ahead of you.

That's why the friends we keep and the choices we make are so important. Hanging out with the wrong crowd can become a nightmare overnight. Make decisions that work for you. Build on your reputation as someone not afraid to do the right thing. Integrity is a vital ingredient to your future.

Read this book to suit your lifestyle. You might want to leave it on your bedside table and read a few entries before ending your day. Use the Internet and the library to learn more about these men. Hopefully, you'll discover new heroes and be inspired by their stories.

Think of *The Boldness of Boys* as your primer, a sampling of biographies of men who've made a difference in this world just by doing what they love to do. Learn from them. Add your own spin to their ideas. All of these men want to help you figure it out. They were eager for their stories to be profiled here because they want the next generation to benefit from their experiences. It's their own way of paying it forward.

So push the envelope, take risks, and think outside the box. This is your life, your adventure to pursue. I invite you to spend some time with the real-life heroes featured in *The Boldness of Boys*. Then get started on your own heroic journey.

With my admiring respect,
Susan Strong

THE CAPE

Eight years old with a flour sack cape
Tied all around his neck
He climbed up on the garage
Figurin' what the heck
He screwed his courage up so tight
The whole thing came unwound
He got a runnin' start and bless his heart
He headed for the ground

He's one of those who knows that life
Is just a leap of faith
Spread your arms and hold your breath
Always trust your cape

All grown up with a flour sack cape
Tied around his dreams
He's full of piss and vinegar
He's bustin' at the seams
He licked his finger and checked the wind
It's gonna be do or die
He wasn't scared of nothin', Boys
He was pretty sure he could fly

He's one of those who knows that life
Is just a leap of faith
Spread your arms and hold your breath
Always trust your cape

Old and grey with a flour sack cape
Tied all around his head
He's still jumpin' off the garage
And will be till he's dead
All these years the people said
He's actin' like a kid
He did not know he could not fly
So he did

—Guy Clark, Susanna Clark, and Jim Janosky

THE BOLDNESS OF BOYS

CHAPTER 1

ADRENALINE HIGH

Unleashing Your Talents

> There are admirable potentialities in every human being. Believe in your strength and your youth. Learn to repeat endlessly to yourself, "It all depends on me."
>
> —ANDRÉ GIDE

It's your comfort zone times twenty. It's how you choose to spend your time. You get light-headed once homework is done and the time is now yours to do what you want. Your adrenaline does the talking for you and says, "This is it, man."

Often in life, what we are most interested in at an early age stays with us. But even if it leaves for a while, when it comes back, that same adrenaline high comes back with it, a rush that jolts your brain and screams, "This feels awesome!"

3

This chapter tells stories about men recognizing their own talents: Wayne Gretzky, hopelessly addicted to hockey; Dave Barry, class clown from the start; Roald Dahl, spent hours making up stories; Neil Leifer, early shutterbug.

They remember the high they experienced the first time they really felt their passion. They also remember the lessons learned from taking a chance.

It's not always obvious or easy, but if you pay attention to what feels honest to your core, you are probably on the right track. Don't expect yourself right now to know what you want to do when you grow up. You are still in the planning stages. This time in life is about experiencing that adrenaline rush. Act on it or file it away for later. Whatever you chose, have fun and enjoy the magic of unleashing your own talents.

TONY HAWK
Professional Skateboarder
born: 1968

 WHY TONY

Because the man virtually flies upside down while a skateboard stays glued to his feet.

Because Tony Hawk became a household name and introduced the world to professional skateboarding. Hawk went pro at the age of fourteen and by sixteen was the best skateboarder in the world. He's the master of such daunting moves as the ollie 540, the kickflip 540, the varial 720, and the 900.

Because in 1999, Hawk landed the first-ever 900 (two and a half midair spins) at the Summer X Games.

Though Tony Hawk never thought he could make a career out of skateboarding, that didn't stop him from skating, falling, and crashing at Oasis Skatepark near his home in San Diego. He created moves in the air that no one thought possible. Tony knew when he was young that he was born to board. From an early age, he was a self-proclaimed troublemaker, but got focused once he discovered the adrenaline high of skateboarding. When his underdeveloped body caught up with his intellect, there was no stopping him. His father supported his passion by building ramps and driving Tony up and down the California coast in search of the best competitions. When Tony's dad became dissatisfied with the limited level of competition, he founded the California Amateur Skateboard League.

TONY'S STORY:

One day I saw an issue of *Skateboarder* magazine, and it changed my life. Imagine, a magazine dedicated to skateboarding! But it wasn't the skateboarding that sucked me in; *Skateboarder* had pictures of amateur kids from all around the world ripping. Oasis had more than its fair share of insane skaters; in fact, two of the '70s best pro skaters in the world were locals, Steve Cathey and Dave Andrecht. Dave was one of the burliest skaters in the world at the time. Steve was a more clean-cut guy with a smooth style. They both lived in San Diego and had pictures in my first issue of *Skateboarder*. That was as famous as anybody could get for me.

My dad would pick me up at Oasis to bring me to basketball practice. One day, when we were running late, I rushed onto the court. I was ready to play. I hadn't realized I still had my kneepads on. As I sat on the bench to remove my pads, I looked at my dad. I knew I had to come out of the closet and tell him I didn't want to play any more team sports. The only thing I really liked besides skateboarding was playing the violin. In my brain, skateboarding and playing the violin didn't seem that different, because they were individual pursuits. I sucked in a deep breath and looked at the floor. "Dad, I'd rather skate than play basketball. I'm having more fun skating, and I feel like getting better."

I thought he'd get upset. He was one of the coaches, after all, and the association had just elected him Little League president. I pretended to be messing around with my pads as I waited for the pep talk, but my dad had realized a long time before what skating meant to me.

"Fine by me," he answered, and my career as a jock officially ended.

ROBERT BALLARD
Explorer, Oceanographer

born: 1942

❓ WHY ROBERT

Because as president of the Institute for Exploration in Mystic, Connecticut, Robert Ballard and his team located the *Titanic* in 1985.

Because the interest in the *Titanic* from children was so overwhelming, he created the Jason Project, an educational organization that teaches kids about his expeditions through live video-feeds beamed over the Internet to more than 200,000 million students. Because he's made over 100 deep-sea expeditions, discovering other shipwrecks like the *Bismarck,* the *Yorktown,* the *Lusitania,* and the famous *PT-109* from World War II.

Because Ballard believes in curating his discoveries and leaving everything as he and his team found it.

Because he's still learning and teaching others at the University of Rhode Island, Graduate School of Oceanography.

Spending time in a confined space is fun to Robert Ballard, as long as it's a submersible unit that takes him exploring through the ocean. His enthusiasm is infectious. Kids worldwide are catching his passion about the power of the sea and what lies beneath. His robotic designs can be motored on land as well as cruise the ocean floor.

It's no surprise Ballard was the man who finally found the lost *Titanic*. He caught the ocean bug during high school when he enrolled in a scholarship program at the Scripps Institution in San Diego. Upon graduation from high school, he attended the University of California, Santa Barbara, and majored in physical science, a degree that allowed him to study the underwater world.

ROBERT'S STORY:

Growing up, the ocean was my playground. I was lucky because I grew up in the '50s, after World War II and before Vietnam, an era when America could do anything, including going to the moon.

I was born in 1942 and my father was a test pilot during the war. My dad was head of the Minuteman Missile Program, worked for North American Aviation, and was on the team that built the *Apollo*.

I was caught up in the "there isn't anything we can't do" attitude that prevailed back then. I'm sure that's how the seed to explore the ocean was planted. So I became an oceanographer and a naval officer.

The pivotal point in my life was that scholarship to Scripps when I was in high school. I was seventeen, living in Los Angeles at the time, and a junior in high school. Because I grew up near Scripps, I knew it was the place to be. They had an aquarium and all that. I wrote this letter to the institution that basically said, "Dear Santa, I want to be an oceanographer. What do I do?" Instead of it not being answered, a man named Norris Rigstraw wrote back. He was a dean there. He told me about the scholarship program and included an

9

application. I filled it out and I got this scholarship. In the summer of 1959, at age seventeen, I went to sea. They sent me on a true oceanographic expedition. I fell in love with the adventure. Many people do fun-seeking and daredevil stuff, but I was searching for a purpose. That summer I found it. I wanted to be an explorer. I wanted to accomplish something. I wasn't interested in bungee jumping off some bridge.

DAVE BARRY
Humor Columnist
born: 1947

? WHY DAVE

Because Dave Barry writes a newspaper column about ordinary events that makes readers laugh out loud at the absurdities of life.

Because Barry's Pulitzer Prize–winning humor column is syndicated nationally in over 500 newspapers.

Because he still wonders how that happened.

Because he has also written twenty-four books, including *Big Trouble,* which was made into a motion picture.

When not writing about important world events and social issues—like exploding toilets—Dave Barry plays in a literary rock band that includes Stephen King as a member. Barry describes the band as low on talent but high on noise. A self-proclaimed nerd in childhood, Barry figured the best way to win friends was to humor them. It worked and jump-started his career as a humorist.

DAVE'S STORY:

I grew up in a little town in suburban New York City called Armonk, which today is another address in the megaburbs of New York. But when I grew up, it was a small town of only about 2,000 people. Pretty much everyone knew everyone, which was good and bad. It was mostly good, because you felt safe in this sort of a classic American childhood. You did occasionally get caught blowing up somebody's mailbox with a cherry bomb. And the person whose mailbox you blew up was very likely to know your father real well. So there was always that issue—not to say that I ever blew up anyone's mailbox. But I may have been there when it happened.

I was the classic person due to become a humor columnist in the sense that I was small, puny, not athletic, a late bloomer. I hit puberty when I was about thirty. I was the first kid to get glasses, I had a giant forehead, and my father cut my hair. All of these things conspired to make me *not* the Brad Pitt of Wompus Elementary School. So I was the classic nerd. I used humor to make friends and to deflect any attention from my high forehead. It was made official when I was elected class clown. I was always the kid telling jokes.

For the most part, my humor saved me. You could argue that I was actually fairly popular for my puniness. And it did sort of form the basis of how I related to everybody from then on, which was by making fun of everything and believing no one would really like me if I wasn't funny.

I tended to have one really close friend and sort of got along with everybody else. That was until I started to get interested in girls. It hit home when I was in about sixth grade. It was the year girls went to bosom camp at the end of fifth grade and came back and, Whoa! What's that! It became harder to have good friendships with other guys for a while, because we were all so busy being stupid trying to figure out how to get the girls to like us. I really wanted the girls to be interested in me and they weren't. And so because I was only interested in girls, my early adolescence strikes me as the worst time in my life. I was so clueless, so confused, and I didn't have any confidence at all. And, of course, everybody's really cruel, including you, because you're trying so hard to be cool. It was just god-awful.

And throughout this time I always liked to write, and I especially liked to write humor. I was always interested in my educational career, but I had to pretend that I wasn't just so I could still be friends with the larger, hairier, more muscle-y boys. They would have beaten me up for being a good writer. I just remember junior high as being a bad time. Things got better in high school.

MARTIN RICHARDS
Broadway and Film Producer

born: 1932

? WHY MARTIN

Because Martin Richards has the magic touch. A producer extraordinaire of stage and screen, his most recent mega Broadway play and film production of *Chicago* was nominated for eleven Tony Awards and won six Academy Awards.

Because as head of the film and theatrical company the Producer's Circle, he has produced runaway hits on stage, including *On the Twentieth Century, Sweeney Todd, The Will Rogers Follies,* and *La Cage Aux Folles,* all of which earned numerous awards. His films include *The Shining, The Boys from Brazil,* and *Fort Apache, the Bronx.*

Because Martin Richards doesn't just produce great entertainment, he produces much goodwill. He has cofounded a medical center for organ transplantation and research and a nonprofit organization for abused children, and he sits on many boards supporting the arts culture in New York City.

Whether he was serenading his neighborhood from his fire escape in the Bronx or belting out tunes on the Broadway stage, Martin Richards loved singing, though it was not easy to admit to his "jock" friends at school. Making them laugh was easier. At the beginning of his career, throat polyps forced him to quit singing professionally and that's when he turned his attention to finding quality plays and films to produce. Today, the process of producing gets Martin Richards excited, but in his youth, it was the rush of being on stage.

MARTIN'S STORY:

My mother always said, "My darling son, yours was such an easy birth but you made up for it the rest of your life." I was really always searching for my way in the world. I was like a fish out of water in my neighborhood. Yet, I was very popular. It helped that my mother brought homemade cookies to school for every holiday and she really made sure I was never shy.

It was a different time then. Neighbors knew neighbors. Families were very tight. If your kid was in trouble, three other families jumped in to call your parents.

I was labeled a dreamer in school. I loved to sing more than anything so I always sang in the hallway on the sixth floor of my building. One day, our next-door neighbor, Mrs. Wax, told my mother, "You know, Cheryl, your son has a terrific voice. Why don't you give him voice lessons?" So when I was about seven, my dad took me to the Marie Moses School of Song & Dance. I ended up signing in many kids' musical shows as well as on television and in a few commercials.

I just sang. It's what I did. People would say, "He's a singer; he's going to be a star." In fact, growing up, my brother used to say to me, "All right, Star, there's no camera on. Go wash the bathtub." It was very strange because at the time I was singing until I was even in my early teens, no one talked about it. When I wasn't working, I hung out in the poolroom with the rest of the guys. I knew better than to talk about singing and dancing because I would have been labeled a sissy. So automatically I started to develop a neurosis like, "Oh my gosh, what kind of freaky business am I in?"

Oddly enough, I was always trying to fit it, yet I never had a problem because I covered up my insecurities by being the class comic and getting into trouble. I was voted the most popular in both my junior and senior year of high school. I was always making fun of myself. Here I was, this singing fool surrounded by all these big jocks. I wouldn't focus on my singing; instead I depended on my humor. It wasn't until I was older that I truly found my place. I learned that I didn't have to be ashamed of what I love to do. Looking back, I don't know why I was ashamed in the first place. Nobody made me feel that way.

I thrived when I was on that stage. Though I'd get very nervous and even nauseous beforehand, once I got over the first-number jitters, no matter how old I was, the applause just enveloped me. Nothing gave me that incredible feeling again until I won my first Tony Award.

MILTON GLASER

Graphic Designer

born: 1929

❓ WHY MILTON

Because the master of graphic design's "I Love [heart symbol] NY" logo has become an internationally recognized icon.

Because Milton Glaser's vision and design sense compel us to pick up certain items in stores.

Because his work has appeared in museums and private collections all over the world.

Often referred to as the "Picasso of the graphic arts field," Milton Glaser's designs deliver his message through art more than words.

His talent emerged early and was nurtured at New York City's High School of Music and Art. The creative environment offered students the opportunity to develop their talents in art or music while completing a comprehensive academic program.

Making art kept Glaser company during a childhood that was somewhat isolated and lonely due to a life-changing event.

MILTON'S STORY:

When I was eight, I contracted rheumatic fever. I was hospitalized for several months and then had to stay in bed for almost a year. I think when an event like that occurs in childhood, it sort of pulls you out of the general current of your life and isolates you, forcing you to go inward in some way. You immediately recognize that you're not attached to life like other children are. To be sort of psychological about it, an event of that kind produces significant consequences. I remember that time in my life as being very profound. It made me turn inward. That's probably when I decided to become an artist. I realized I would have to amuse myself. I began to build little cities and create armies. Every day, I would take several pounds of clay and create a little universe and then destroy it at the end of the day and the next day start over. There was power in doing that and it kept me entertained. The act of making things became more important than anything else. It confirmed an internal decision about how I would spend my life.

LANCE ARMSTRONG

World, National, and Olympic Champion Cyclist

born: 1971

❓ WHY LANCE

Because nobody rides a bike better, longer, faster, than Lance Armstrong.

Because he brought home five (1999, 2000, 2001, 2002, 2003) Tour de France trophies.

Because the man with true grit found the toughest challenge in 1996, when he was diagnosed with testicular cancer that had spread to his lungs and brain.

Because he's not a quitter; he's a survivor who takes on challenges and likes to win.

Because he created the Lance Armstrong Foundation, which benefits cancer research and focuses on helping people manage and survive cancer.

It was a Schwinn Mag Scrambler, Lance's first set of wheels, at age seven. By age sixteen, he had turned pro, competing in triathlons. By then, the bike had won out as his best friend. His hometown, Plano, Texas, was perfect biking country. He rode and rode until . . . "Hello, Mom, can you pick me up? I rode to Oklahoma!" Lance's passion became unleashed when he was free to roam.

LANCE'S STORY:

One afternoon when I was about 13 and hanging around the Richardson Bike Mart, I saw a flyer for a competition called IronKids. It was a junior triathlon, an event that combined biking, swimming, and running. I had never heard of a triathlon before—but it was all of the things

I was good at, so I signed up. My mother took me to a shop and bought me a triathlon outfit, which basically consisted of cross-training shorts and a shirt made out of a hybrid fast-drying material, so I could wear it through each phase of the event, without changing. We got my first racing bike then, too. It was a Mercier, a slim, elegant road bike.

I won, and I won by a lot, without even training for it. Not long afterward, there was another triathlon, in Houston. I won that, too. When I came back from Houston, I was full of self-confidence. I was a top junior at swimming, but I had never been the absolute best at it. I was better at triathlons than any kid in Plano, and any kid in the whole state, for that matter. I liked the feeling.

What makes a great endurance athlete is the ability to absorb potential embarrassment, and to suffer without complaint. I was discovering that if it was a matter of gritting my teeth, not caring how it looked, and outlasting everybody else, I won. It didn't matter what sport. In straight-ahead, long-distance races, I could beat anybody.

If it was a suffer-fest, I was good at it.

CHARLES CHAMPLIN

Writer, Former Film Critic and Talk-Show Host

born: 1926

❓WHY CHARLES

Because he knows celebrities up close and personal. As a reporter for *Time* and *Life* magazines, Charles Champlin wrote about the emerging arts culture in America and abroad.

Because while living in London, he suggested to *Time* magazine that they run a story about a little-known band called the Beatles. *Time* magazine passed on the request, and a year later, the Beatles invaded America.

Because as the author of over ten books, Champlin has written about the careers of his friends Alfred Hitchcock, George Lucas, John Frankenheimer, and Woody Allen.

Because he was the film critic and arts editor for the *Los Angeles Times* for three decades, and was the host of *Champlin on Film,* a TV series on Bravo, featuring guests such as Dustin Hoffman, Danny Glover, Tom Hanks, Hugh Grant, and Jodie Foster.

Charles Champlin's candid and graceful style is an expected luxury in the life of his readers. In his youth, books kept him company and provided a fantasy life, taking him places far from his small town. For pocket change, Champlin had a paper route, driving his bike around town delivering papers to anyone who would buy them from him. All that time alone let him dream about what could be. And the primary dream always involved him writing.

CHARLES'S STORY:

All those hours on the bicycle, like the winter hours I spent reading on an ancient wicker chaise-lounge in my bedroom, were perfect for developing a fantasy life. For reasons that even now I can't quite account for, the richest and most persistent fantasy I had was of becoming a writer. So far as I'm aware there had never been a writer in the family on either side, although there had been plenty of enthusiastic readers. I didn't know any writers or any aspiring writers. Yet again and again I saw myself sitting at the typewriter, puffing a pipe, withdrawing checks from envelopes, seeing my words in print. I also fantasized about hitting home runs and playing cornet solos of unbelievable brilliance, but those fantasies were so thoroughly unbelievable that I wasted very little time on them.

A friend of mine once asked Robert Frost when he decided he was a poet. Frost said, "My dear, when did you decide you were a beautiful woman?" He meant that there was no conscious decision involved, only a recognition of a truth that was inescapable. I've said, and I think it's true, that your first tip-off that there may be writing in your future comes very early. It is, let's say, a little easier for you than for some of your pals to write those awful thank-you notes at Christmas time for the box of handkerchiefs you'd always wanted (or, as was more likely the case, hadn't). I was a whiz at thank-you notes and I could type long before I was ten. After that I was just following the lines of least resistance.

And so as I stumbled toward adolescence I was already becoming a cliché: the would-be writer whose richest life is led in the imagination, fired by radio, movies, books, pulp magazines, and all that solitude.

NEIL LEIFER
Photojournalist

born: 1942

? WHY NEIL

Because so many famous sports photos have been taken by Neil Leifer.

Because since 1960, over 200 of his images have graced the covers of *Sports Illustrated, Time,* and *People* magazines, making him the most published photojournalist in Time, Inc., history.

Because for fifteen Olympic Games, every gold-medal winner has been the focus of Leifer's lens.

Neil Leifer is precise and thorough to the core. Was he born this way, or did growing up on the streets of New York's Lower East Side factor into his determined spirit? He credits an after-school program for teaching him photography. From there, the sky was the limit.

NEIL'S STORY:

I grew up in Manhattan in the late '40s, when the Lower East Side was considered the great melting pot of America. It's where immigrants came in search of a better life. Our neighborhood was poor. Many were uneducated blue-collar workers who tried to give their children what they didn't have. My mother came from Poland because of the Holocaust. Most of her family perished. My father was born on the Lower East Side. His parents were Russian immigrants. My dad was a postal employee. The neighborhood was Irish, Italian, and Jewish. There was an expression in the old neighborhood that half the kids went up the river to prisons like Sing Sing and the other half became the lawyers and judges who sent them there. So opportunity did exist. The public schools were wonderful. Any kid who didn't get an education was a kid who didn't want one. Along with the opportunity to learn was the opportunity to get in trouble.

To keep kids from throwing away their lives on crime or drugs, we had settlement houses. I joined one called the Henry Street Settlement House that still stands today. It's over a hundred years old. A variety of programs, from boxing and the Golden Gloves to other sports like basketball and baseball, were offered. You could also learn how to play an instrument. All the classes were free.

Henry House also had a camera club that was taught by a wonderful woman named Nellie. She was a Russian immigrant who was an inspiration to us all. No one could afford equipment, so cameras—small box cameras with a Brownie Hawkeye—were donated by various companies. Film was donated, too. Because there was only so much equipment to go around, we rotated days. We'd go out into the neighborhood, shoot a roll of film, and bring it in on our designated day, when Nellie would teach us how to develop film into negatives. Then we'd make prints of our work. Every Christmas, Nellie held a photo contest and offered a prize to the winner. I never won, but she inspired a love of photography that, in my case, obviously lasted.

My interest in photographing navy ships and planes began back then. I would read in the paper that some navy ships were coming into the West Side piers and go over there so I could photograph them. I remember photographing the battleship *New Jersey*. Twenty years later, I photographed that same ship in Vietnam for *Life* magazine.

By the time I entered high school, I was a photo enthusiast. I owned a very inexpensive camera that I may have gotten for my bar mitzvah. My father thought this was a rich man's hobby but did buy me an inexpensive enlarger, and before too long, I had a darkroom set up in my bathroom so I could develop film whenever I wanted to.

In high school, I was a photographer and picture editor for the school newspaper. That's when I began taking sports photos. Lots of photographers are content to take wonderful pictures, but I always wanted to see mine published. I always got a big bang out of seeing my name next to my photograph, and, believe it or not, I still do today.

KELLY SLATER
World Champion Surfer
born: 1972

? WHY KELLY

Because he's number one, the man to beat. No one compares to this winner of six surfing world titles.

Because he took time off in 1990 to get even smarter and now he's back on the board, riding waves, winning competitions, with his new thirty-year-old perspective.

Known as "the Boss," Kelly Slater's approach is cerebral, his execution pure gymnastics. Cocoa Beach, Florida, is home and where Slater learned his art on calmer seas. He compares surfing in Florida to walking; you learn to walk before you run. The urge to compete came at a young age.

KELLY'S STORY:

I grew up in Cocoa Beach, Florida. I lived there with my parents and my older and younger brothers. My dad was a surfer and owned a bait and tackle store near the beach, so our whole lives were based around the ocean and the river.

Elementary school was pretty normal. I had other interests like baseball, basketball, football, and tennis, but most of my time was spent surfing. My dad used to coach my football team, but I would miss practices to go surfing. The coach was there; his son wasn't.

When I was ten years old, I won my first big event—the East Coast Surfing Championships. I won that six years straight. I actually started competing at age eight. When I was seven, I wanted to compete at this charity event that is still held every year in Cocoa Beach, but my mom said I was too young. I eventually won my first competition there. Only three other kids in the event were in my age group. After winning, I brought my trophy and some pictures to school. I had this teacher; she was black. I was a little scared of her because growing up where I did, I didn't really know any black people. But I really respected her. To this day, she remains my favorite teacher. I remember her telling me, "Don't you brag," when I brought my stuff in. That set me straight. There are always a few people in anyone's life that they remember, who really stand out. She is one.

I went professional when I was a senior in high school. I was eighteen. From age eight on, you couldn't get me out of the water; I was so passionate about waves and the ocean and learning how to surf. Surfing to me is an art—about drawing lines in the waves.

ROALD DAHL
Writer
1916—1990

? WHY ROALD

Because his books are the first ones checked out of the library. Reading becomes an adventure with Ronald Dahl, who wrote *Charlie and the Chocolate Factory, The Twits, Matilda, James and the Giant Peach, Fantastic Mr. Fox, The BFG,* and many more children's books.

Because he's on the kids' side—helping them with difficult and snooty adults, getting them in and out of bizarre situations, and making sure there are plenty of silly details to complete his hysterical stories.

Because it's Dahl's world—quirky and loved by all who read him again and again.

Maybe kids relate to Roald Dahl's stories because he had been documenting his own feelings since childhood; because he was an adult who remembered what it was like to be a kid. To ensure that his nosy sisters didn't read his diary, he locked it in a tin box and tied it to the top of a tree. Writing daily prepared him for his career as a writer. By the time he was raising his own children, his mind was a treasure box of stories, which he told again and again.

He remembered his childhood as lonely, mostly because of time spent in boarding schools, which his mother preferred over the schools in Llandaff, Wales. In one school, Repton, he would recall the mouthwatering experience that planted the seed for one of his most famous books.

ROALD'S STORY:

Every now and again, a plain grey cardboard box was dished out to each boy in our House, and this, believe it or not, was a present from the great chocolate manufacturers, Cadbury. Inside the box there were twelve bars of chocolate, all of different shapes, all with different fillings and all with numbers from one to twelve stamped on the chocolate underneath. Eleven of these bars were new inventions from the factory. The twelfth was the "control" bar, one that we all knew well, usually a Cadbury's Coffee Cream bar. Also in the box was a sheet of paper with the numbers one to twelve on it as well as two blank columns, one for giving marks to each chocolate from nought to ten, and the other for comments.

All we were required to do in return for this splendid gift was to taste very carefully each bar of chocolate, give it marks and make an intelligent comment on why we liked it or disliked it. . . .

. . . For me, the importance of all this was that I began to realize that the large chocolate companies actually did possess inventing rooms and they took their inventing very seriously. I used to picture a long white room like a laboratory with pots of chocolate and fudge and all sorts of other delicious fillings bubbling away on the stoves, while men and women in white coats moved between the bubbling pots, tasting and mixing and con-cocting their wonderful new inventions. I used to imag-ine myself working in one of these labs and suddenly I would come up with something so absolutely unbearably delicious that I would grab it in my hand and go rushing out of the lab and along the corridor and right into the office of the great Mr. Cadbury himself. "I've got it, sir!" I would shout, putting the chocolate in front of him. "It's fantastic! It's fabulous! It's marvelous! It's irresistible!"

Slowly, the great man would pick up my newly invented chocolate and he would take a small bite. He would roll it round his mouth. Then all at once, he would leap up from his chair . . . slap me on the back and shout, "We'll sell it by the million! We'll sweep the world with this one! How on earth did you do it? Your salary is doubled!"

It was lovely dreaming those dreams, and I have no doubt at all that, thirty-five years later, when I was looking for a plot for my second book for children, I remembered those little cardboard boxes for the newly invented chocolates inside them, and I began to write a book called *Charlie and the Chocolate Factory*.

JAMES BURKE
Business Innovator

born: 1925

? WHY JAMES

Because when he was president and chief executive officer of Johnson & Johnson (the Tylenol, baby powder, and Band-Aid company), millions of Americans panicked when seven people died after taking Tylenol capsules that were laced with cyanide. Burke pulled every bottle of Tylenol off the shelves and immediately established triple-seal packaging on all bottles.

Because his ethical actions became the model that corporate America follows when dealing with crises.

Because of his concern for this country's drug problem, he sat as the unpaid chairman of the board of Partnership for a Drug-Free America for thirteen years.

Because in 2000, James Burke received the Presidential Medal of Freedom, the nation's highest civil honor.

James Burke had a mind for business at an early age. Maybe it was because his parents encouraged him and his siblings to read the daily newspaper and give a report at dinner. At age fourteen, Burke learned the old adage "There's no success like failure," when his first entrepreneurial endeavor backfired.

JAMES'S STORY:

We lived in a place called Slingerlands, New York. I had decided there was good money to be made harvesting and selling Christmas trees, partly because my mother's family lived in an area where I could buy trees for a very good price. My grandfather helped me purchase the trees and get them shipped to where I lived. I figured I could sell 100, so that's what we ordered.

Display and merchandising were my next challenge. There was a little one-room barbershop in town and the barber was a good friend of mine, so I persuaded him to let me set up a lot next to his shop. Part of my pitch was that people who stopped by to purchase a tree might also need a haircut. He agreed to my proposition, and though he didn't ask for commission, I'd planned to compensate him.

The trees arrived and looked wonderful. The local media made a story out of it and it turned into a great success initially. Each morning before school, I'd stop by the lot, but on the third day when I arrived, all the trees were gone.

It turned out that the barber was a raging alcoholic, a fact everyone but me seemed to know. He'd work all day and drink himself to sleep. While he was in a stupor, the trees were stolen. It taught me a lot. I never trusted people quite as much as I had before that incident.

It doesn't end there, because I still had to pay for the cost of the trees. I had to find a way to raise money. Initially, I sold door-to-door stuff like magazines and newspapers, until a field of daffodils spawned a new idea. There was this big mansion in our town that had a small horse track, where the owners rode their horses. In the middle of that track grew the largest field of daffodils I had ever seen. I suggested to the owner that I sell the daffodils, which she had no interest in until I told her that I would give her 50 percent of whatever I made. Another friend let me sell them on his property, provided I cut him in on the deal, and I gladly did that, too. We cut and wrapped them in green paper and displayed them on a big stand by the highway. And we sold them by the dozens. I recouped all the money I lost on the trees and had a new business venture I capitalized on for the next two years. However, I never did sell Christmas trees again.

PETER LORD
Animator
born: 1953

? WHY PETER

Because Peter Lord is the artist who creates the clay models in animated films like *Chicken Run* and the popular and clever cartoon episodes of *Wallace & Gromit*.

Because as the cofounder of Aardman Animations, he creates each character slowly and with patience, until each move is just right.

Peter Lord started animating for fun with his school chum David Sproxton (cofounder of Aardman). Their whimsical storyboards and chalkline drawings took off almost immediately after a friend's father aired them on England's TV network, the BBC. Influenced by his artistic family, Peter learned to trust his talent, though he didn't think he could make a living doing what came naturally.

PETER'S STORY:

I think I knew when I was about six that I was an artist and perhaps a storyteller, too. I always liked writing stories in school, and because I liked joking around, my friends knew me as the spinner of yarns.

From the start, I drew on my own. My mother was an artist, so I think that's where it came from. I saw my mother painting and I'd paint. I draw. My kids draw. I used to believe these things came from your parents, because that was my experience, but common sense tells you that that can't be true for the whole world.

By age fifteen, my partner David Sproxton and I started animating as a hobby. Animating is so exciting to do. It allows you to create this moment, normally quite a short moment, and it's absolutely entirely your own creation. You make something happen. Even something really simple like making a man out of modeling clay that walks across the set and falls down an invisible hole. To make that happen, you slice the clay up to make it appear that he's fallen down the hole. And when you're doing that, you're sitting in a room with maybe the radio playing, a cup of tea, and your modeling clay. Six hours pass without you noticing because what you're doing is so interesting and challenging. It's all about you and the modeling clay, and that's all. But when you finish, that man is walking across the set and falling into an invisible hole. And you know it never happened. It's magic you made happen. It's such a strong, pure feeling of creation that when you see it, you think, "Wow! That was great."

That's what we thought when we were fifteen. And then we pushed it further and needed some help. We needed to make a connection at the BBC. We did. Frankly, it was nepotism. Knowing someone really helps. The guy at the BBC didn't tell us to throw in the towel. He saw our work, which was very, very primitive, and he said, "Do some more and maybe I'll buy it." So we did, and he bought several for fifteen pounds or something like that, not much money at all. But now we're seventeen years old and our work is on television. So that was our start. Initially, the excitement was purely personal, the excitement of creation.

WAYNE GRETZKY

Former Professional Hockey Player

born: 1961

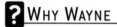 ## WHY WAYNE

Because Wayne Gretzky dominated the National Hockey League (NHL) for twenty seasons.

Because he helped Canada's Edmonton Oilers win four Stanley Cup Championships.

Because Gretzky rules as leader in goals and assists, and when he was traded to the Los Angeles Kings, he made hockey a major sports attraction in California for seven seasons.

Because of his greatness, when Gretzky retired in 1999 from the New York Rangers, his jersey number (99) was retired, too, a first in the NHL.

Still referred to as "The Great One," today Wayne Gretzky is a managing partner of the Phoenix Coyotes and is in charge of all hockey operations. The seeds of his greatness were planted young. At age four, he began to skate in his hometown, Brantford, Ontario. By age ten, Wayne finished the season with 378 goals and 120 assists in 85 games in the Brantford atom league.

He was fortunate that his passion to play was always supported by his parents. Whenever asked how athletes become good, Gretzky's reply is always the same: "Practice, practice, practice."

WAYNE'S STORY:

I had a serious addiction to hockey. I'd drag my dad over to the park every day and make him sit out there freezing his buns until bedtime. He finally got so cold he did something crazy. He turned our backyard into a hockey rink. The Wally Coliseum. The first time he did it I was four. He cut the grass down real short in the fall, waited until the ground froze, covered it with a half-inch of snow, set the sprinkler in the middle and turned it on—all night. The backyard is small, so the rink covered it all. People thought he was crazy, but this way he could watch me from the warmth of his seventy-degree kitchen. . . .

All I wanted to do in the winters was be on the ice. I'd get up in the morning, skate from 7:00 to 8:30, go to school, come home at 3:30, stay on the ice until my mom insisted I come in for dinner, eat in my skates, then go back out until 9:00. On Saturdays and Sundays, we'd have huge games, but nighttime became my time. It was sort of an unwritten rule around the neighborhood that I was to be out there by myself or with my dad. I would just handle the puck in and out of these empty detergent bottles my dad set up as pylons. Then I'd set up targets in the net and try to hit them with forehands, backhands, whatever. Then I'd do it all again, except this time with a tennis ball, which is much harder to handle.

I was so addicted that my dad had big kids come over to play against me. And when the kids wanted to go home, I'd beg them to stay longer. I suppose that's how I was always able to do well against bigger guys later on. That's all I could get to play against. . . .

Nowadays, people come up to me, dragging their kids behind them, and say, "Wayne, tell my son to practice three hours a day like you did." And I always say, "I'm not going to tell them to practice three hours a day. Let him go ride his bike if he wants." Nobody told me to practice three hours a day. I practiced all day because I loved it. All my friends would leave the ice and say, "Let's go to the movies," but I never wanted to. The only way a kid is going to practice is if it's total fun for him—and it was for me.

CHAPTER 2

PARENTAL UNITS

Can You Relate?

> When I was a boy of fourteen, my father was so ignorant I could hardly stand to have the old man around. But when I got to twenty-one, I was astonished at how much he had learned in seven years.
>
> —MARK TWAIN

Believe it or not, your parents know you pretty well. They've been checking you out since day one. They know your tastes, your habits, your temper. They even claim to know when you are cold—though you might not be—so jam the sweatshirt in your backpack! It'll make your mom happy.

You are your parental units' biggest accomplishment. They have high hopes that you might achieve what they never did. They want you to be able to stand strong and forge your own way in this world. They know that right now is the time to start that journey. It's time for you to become more independent: Make your own lunch, decide how much you can handle after school, clean your own room, and make your own decisions. The time is now to learn responsibility.

With any luck, you are already well on your way to independence, and that's both good and bad. Good because it feels awesome to be in control of your life—to listen to your own music and hang with your friends. Bad because your parents will still say when they don't approve of the decisions you're making.

The men profiled in this chapter of *The Boldness of Boys* generally found guidance and support from their parents. Behind them stood moms and dads guiding and cheering—parents who delivered their first lessons about doing the right thing, the importance of good character, and tolerance of others.

We all have stories to tell about our parents. Stories about them that drive us crazy or make us love them more. Stories that tell a lot about them. What about your parents? Are they good listeners? Are they too demanding? Do they make you feel smothered?

Unable to express yourself? For instance, if you wanted to go to another school, would your parents send you, or would you be too afraid to ask? Telling your parents how you feel, talking about your concerns, can reap unexpected rewards. Write it down first. You might be surprised by what you have to say. Then share it with them. Try it!

You might like it.

MARTIN LUTHER KING, JR.

Civil Rights Leader, Pastor

1929–1968

❓WHY MARTIN

Because he was the leader of America's greatest non-violent movement for justice, equality, and peace.

Because Martin Luther King, Jr., had a dream that people would not be judged by the color of their skin but by the content of their character.

Because through his selfless devotion, he taught others to celebrate human worth by offering black people and the poor hope and a sense of dignity.

Because he received the Nobel Peace Prize in 1964 at the age of thirty-five, the youngest man, second American, and third African American to be so honored.

Because a national holiday is observed in honor of his January 15 birthday. Martin Luther King, Jr., was assassinated because of his beliefs.

Martin Luther King, Jr., thrived on learning and excelled in the process. After skipping the ninth and twelfth grades in high school, at age fifteen he entered Morehouse College under a special program for gifted students. After graduation, Dr. King studied to be a pastor, just like his father and grandfather before him, and went on to

Crozer Theological Seminary where he received his bachelor of divinity. Always recognized as an outstanding student, Dr. King later received his Ph.D. in theology from Boston University.

During this process, he also became a pastor at his father's church, the Ebenezer Baptist Church in Atlanta, Georgia. His mother was soft-spoken and instilled a sense of self-respect in her three children. Dr. King's father was dynamic, demanding attention and respect which he got from blacks and whites alike when he spoke from the pulpit.

Whatever problems he encountered, Dr. King could always count on his father to help. Dr. Martin Luther King, Jr., was assassinated in 1968. In 1974, his mother was shot to death while playing the organ at the Ebenezer Baptist Church.

MARTIN'S STORY:

My home situation was very congenial. I have a marvelous mother and father. I can hardly remember a time that they ever argued (my father happens to be the kind who just won't argue) or had any great falling out. These factors were highly significant in determining my religious attitudes. It is quite easy for me to think of a God of love mainly because I grew up in a family where love was central and where lovely relationships were ever present. It is quite easy for me to think of the universe as basically friendly mainly because of my uplifting hereditary and environmental circumstances. It is quite easy for me to lean more toward optimism than pessimism about human nature mainly because of my childhood experiences.

In my own life and in the life of a person who is seeking to be strong . . . you are both militant and moderate; you are both idealistic and realistic. And I think that my strong determination for justice comes from the very strong, dynamic personality of my father, and I would hope that the gentle aspect comes from a mother who is very gentle and sweet. . . .

My mother confronted the age-old problem of the Negro parent in America: how to explain discrimination and segregation to a small child. She taught me that I should feel a sense of "somebodiness" but that on the other hand I had to go out and face a system that stared me in the face every day saying you are "less than," you are "not equal to." She told me about slavery and how it ended with the Civil War. She tried to explain the divided system of the South—the segregated schools, restaurants, theaters, housing, the white and colored signs on drinking fountains, waiting rooms, lavatories— as a social condition rather than a natural order. She made it clear that she opposed this system and that I must never allow it to make me feel inferior. Then she said the words that almost every Negro hears before he can yet understand the injustice that makes them necessary: "You are as good as anyone." At this time Mother had no idea that the little boy in her arms would years later be involved in a struggle against the system she was speaking of.

JACKIE CHAN

Actor, Martial Arts Master

born: 1954

? WHY JACKIE

Because this kung fu master who has made over one hundred action films brings his fans big-time thrills with each death-defying move he makes on screen. Whether he's jumping off buildings, hanging from helicopters, or crashing through plate glass windows, Jackie Chan makes audiences gasp at his ability and howl at his jokes.

Because Asia's biggest box office draw and America's adopted son performs his own adrenaline-pumping stunts in action films like *Rush Hour, Shanghai Noon, Shanghai Knights,* and *The Tuxedo.*

Because courage and comedy wrapped in youthful exuberance make Chan a superstar who has already received a Lifetime Achievement Award from MTV and earned a star on Hollywood's Walk of Fame.

After a few years at the China Drama Academy, Jackie Chan was getting used to the physical demands of practicing his martial arts and dance routines. Though the road to stardom was difficult, when Jackie Chan left the Academy, he landed coveted movie roles.

In the earlier years, when his mother still remained in Hong Kong, she would visit the academy, bringing treats and warm water for baths. At first embarrassed by her efforts, Chan later realized his mother's kind efforts were done out of love.

JACKIE'S STORY:

About the only contact I had with the outside world was through my mother, who came to visit me at the academy every single week. At first I loved these visits, because being with Mom was what I missed most when I came to the academy. Lying on the floor and staring at the cracked, white ceiling of the practice hall, I would remember all the nights she'd sung me to sleep, and all of the nice things she'd cook for me. And I would remember how it felt to lie in my lower bunk, knowing that my Mom was in the bed above me—that she and Dad would protect me from any kind of harm.

But strangely enough, after I had been at the academy for several months, my attitude began to change. I'd learn how to survive at the school, and my carefree days on the Peak seemed farther and farther away. When my Mom visited, she brought me candy and snacks, and I eagerly took them and shared them with my friends. But her visits were also times when she showered me with all the affection on me that she saved up during the days she was away. I was a growing boy, and her hugs and kisses humiliated me in front of other students. . . .

In addition to cuddling me like I was still a little child, she'd always baby me in another way I couldn't stand. Along with her sacks of treats, she's also bring large plastic bags of boiling water. Asking Master for a large metal basin, she's pour the bags in and give me a hot bath, scrubbing me down and washing my hair. I was the cleanest kid at school, but also the most embarrassed. After her visits, my clothes damp and my head wrapped in a towel, I'd be cornered by my older brothers, each with something stupid to say. . . .

One day when my mother arrived, bathwater in hand, I grabbed the bags from her and dropped them on the floor. "No bath today, Mom!" I said, "I don't need one. And I especially don't need you to wash me. I'm big enough to wash myself."

My mother looked at me with silent shock. I was always a rude little boy, and I'd always talk back to my father, with the expected results, but I'd never said anything impolite to her. She didn't say anything; just nodded, quietly, and sat down to open the snacks instead. As she was untying the knots that kept the plastic bags closed, I noticed that her hands were raw and red, chafed almost to the point of bleeding. And then I remembered the long walk from the house on the Peak to the bus stop, and the even longer ride down the mountain road, and the lines at the ferry dock, and the crowded, twisting streets from Kowloon terminal to the school.

Mom had boiled the water for the bath in the ambassador's kitchen. And carried it for over an hour to bring it here to me. She did this once a week, every week. And I was telling her that all of her caring and exertion and pain was for nothing.

I pulled her hands away from the bag and hugged her tight. "I'm sorry, Mom," I said. "I . . . I guess I didn't realize how dirty I was. I really could use a bath."

And I smiled up at her. She really was the greatest mother in the world. And she smiled back.

"How was the bath today, honey?" said Yuen Lung, pulling his round face into a mockery of maternal affection.

I looked at him and wrinkled my nose.

"It was great, Big Brother," I said, scrubbing the towel across my wet scalp. "You know, maybe you guys should consider taking one yourselves. 'Cause something really stinks around here."

And as their jaws dropped to the floor, I walked away humming one of mother's songs, towel in one hand, her bag of treats in the other.

ANSEL ADAMS
Photographer, Conservationist
1902–1984

 WHY ANSEL

Because he was the master photographer of the West. Ansel Adams's legendary black-and-white photos of Yosemite National Park and other natural landscapes offer visions of beauty so grand, they have become the standard by which all other nature photos are judged.

Because as a board member of the Sierra Club for nearly forty years, Adams focused on working with the government to preserve national parks.

Because America claimed Ansel Adams as its own national treasure by awarding him the prestigious National Medal of Freedom, the nation's highest civil honor.

Had Ansel Adams attended school today, he probably would have been labeled with attention deficit disorder. School just didn't work for him. He was bored and needed to be outside. Fortunately, his parents agreed. In 1915, Ansel's father withdrew the thirteen-year-old from school and allowed him to attend the World's Fair, the Panama-Pacific International Exposition in San Francisco. Ansel attended daily and thrived on learning about the world in a different way.

ANSEL'S STORY:

My parents enrolled me in a succession of schools. From that early period when I was battling institutional education, I too well remember the Rochambeau School. The architect of the school must have been a dull and primitive cubist. It was a dismal three-story building, dark brown on the outside, dark brown and tan on the inside; everything, including its atmosphere, grimly brown. The students acquired this pervading mood of depression from the teachers, and the teachers must have caught it from the building: big square rooms, wide noisy staircases, grimy windows, ink-stained desks, smudged blackboards, and crummy toilets. The janitor dour, the principal grim, and the playground dirty!

Each day was a severe test for me, sitting in a dreadful classroom while the sun and fog played outside. Most of the information received meant absolutely nothing to me. For example, I was chastised for not being able to remember what states border Nebraska and what are the states of the Gulf Coast. It was simply a matter of memorizing the names, nothing about the *process* of memorizing or any *reason* to memorize. Education without either meaning or excitement is impossible. I longed for the outdoors, leaving only a small part of my conscious self to pay attention to schoolwork.

One day as I sat fidgeting in class the whole situation suddenly appeared very ridiculous to me. I burst into raucous peals of uncontrolled laughter; I could not stop. The class was first amused, then scared. I stood up, pointed at the teacher, and shrieked my scorn, hardly taking breath in between my howling paroxysms. To the dismay of my mother I was escorted home and remained under house arrest for a week until my patient father concluded that my entry into yet another school would be useless. Instead, I was to study at home under his guidance.

After the exposition, my education continued along its individual course. In and out of several schools in search of a legitimizing diploma, I finally ended up at the Wilkins School. Mrs. Kate Wilkins was a stout, motherly character; she read the lessons out loud to me and gave me an A. Graduating from the eighth grade at the Wilkins School signaled the end of my formal academic career.

I often wonder at the strength and courage my father had in taking me out of the traditional school situation and providing me with these extraordinary learning experiences. I am certain he established the positive direction of my life that otherwise, given my native hyperactivity, could have been confused and catastrophic. I trace who I am and the direction of my development to those years of growing up in our house on the dunes, propelled especially by an internal spark tenderly kept alive and glowing by my father.

DEAN SMITH
Former College Basketball Coach
born: 1931

❓ WHY DEAN

Because as the former head coach for the University of North Carolina, Dean Smith won more games than any other coach in basketball history.

Because for thirty-six years, Smith led his team to eleven Final Fours, two national titles, and thirteen ACC Tournament Championships.

Because he is recognized as one of the great minds of basketball, he was respected by his players (96 percent graduated during his tenure), and he managed to win consistently.

Because he taught Michael Jordan how to be a champ.

The Tar Heels at the University of North Carolina at Chapel Hill have an extraordinary basketball record thanks to Coach Dean Smith. Not only did they consistently win during his tenure as head coach, but they also had a friend and confidant in Dean Smith, who always made himself available, inspiring his players to be the best they could be, on and off the court. These valuable life lessons were taught to Smith by his own father.

DEAN'S STORY:

My father was the first real coach I ever knew, and I'm sure I was shaped by him in ways I'm not even conscious of. He taught hygiene and physical education, and in the afternoons he coached football, basketball, baseball, and track. He became head coach for Emporia High in the year I was born, 1931, and the job came with certain pressures. In those days, perhaps even more than now, the entire town was involved with whether the high school team won or lost. Emporia High was a relatively small school of about six hundred students at any given time, and we had to compete against much larger schools from the big cities like Topeka and Wichita, in which we took certain pride. The atmosphere was a lot like the one depicted in the film *Hoosiers*—gymnasiums packed with crowds caught up in the fever pitch of regional rivalries. It was a different game then; the one-handed jump shot hadn't been invented yet, players didn't rise above the rim, and practically everybody used the underhanded scoop shot at the free-throw line.

I suppose you'd call my father a disciplinarian, but the truth is he knew how to get young men, including his son, to behave themselves and to compete hard without having to resort to harsh measures. Take the issue of dinner dishes. Many nights after dinner we would go into the basement and play a game of Ping-Pong. The loser would have to go up and help my mother with the dinner dishes. With the stakes so high, you can imagine how heated the competition was. I made some of the greatest comebacks of my career in that basement. I'd be trailing badly, but the thought of doing dishes would make me frantic. My father would urge me on. "Never give up," he'd say. Somehow I would rally and tie the game. After I'd won, he'd cheerfully tromp back up the stairs and stand at the sink with my mother, his hands in soapy water. We played so often that when I was thirteen, I became the YMCA state champion for my age.

Years later, my father told a Carolina sportswriter

that it was all by design, that he let me back into those games on purpose to teach me the virtue of never quitting. I find it difficult to accept that he let me win. I really believed I mounted those magnificent comebacks on my own. But the more I think about it, there may be something to what he said.

CHRISTOPHER REEVE
Actor, Political Activist
born: 1952

? WHY CHRISTOPHER

Because he will go down in history as playing Superman on the big screen and being a superhero to all his fans, while rehabilitating after a life-altering fall from his horse in 1995 that left him paralyzed.

Because he founded the Christopher Reeve Paralysis Foundation, a leader in finding a cure for paralysis and in bettering the lives of the physically challenged.

Because Christopher Reeve is a hero who found the strength to pursue and endure despite overwhelming obstacles.

Christopher Reeve's parents divorced when he was young, and the impact left him trying to please both sides. He was desperate for his father Franklin's approval and yearned for more time with him. His stepfather, Tris, took an immediate interest and tried to give him direction. He remembers these years as trying times.

CHRISTOPHER'S STORY:

The idea of home was confusing to me, too, because I had grown up between two families, and neither one ever seemed truly secure. This contributed to my developing a fierce independence, which had many positive aspects. But a part of me always looked longingly at other families, where there was communication, respect, and unconditional love, which provided a solid foundation for the children as they grew up.

But as I grew up I felt torn between my parents' quite different and opposed worlds. My father's house was filled with books and visiting intellectuals and stimulating conversation; my mother and stepfather's comfortable house often seemed dull by comparison.

Tris was generous and relaxed, a kind man who always wanted the best for us. He thought it would be better for Ben and me to go to the private school of his childhood—Princeton Country Day, down near Carnegie Lake behind the playing fields of the university. In the fall of 1961 I started in first form, the equivalent of fourth grade. I loved it. On Monday nights we went to father-son carpentry workshops, where we'd build little birdhouses together. Tris came to watch my soccer and hockey games. I developed a great affection for him. Yet this was complicated by the fact that what I wanted most was my father's approval.

So I put a lot of pressure on myself. My mother would say later that I was always straining to be older than I was. It was as if I were trying to race through my childhood, to get it over with. I remember this desire from as far back as the age of six, wanting to read more difficult books, not only because the older kids did but because my father was always surrounded by books, always studying, always writing. Later on the scholar's image became problematic because I wasn't very good in math. But for many years I excelled academically, and that gave me a certain standing with my father, which I needed.

JEAN-MICHEL COUSTEAU

Explorer, Environmentalist, Educator, Film Producer

born: 1938

❓ WHY JEAN-MICHEL

Because as the son of world-famous ocean explorer Jacques Cousteau, he takes seriously his responsibility to continue his father's pioneering work in ocean exploration.

Because as the founder of Ocean Futures Society, Jean-Michel Cousteau serves as "a voice of the ocean," educating students, conducting research, and producing films that promote awareness about the environment.

Jean-Michel Cousteau is the first to admit that he had a privileged youth. He grew up in the south of France and spent much of his time on his father's boat, the *Calypso*. His family traveled all over the world while his father documented the underwater world on film. With no phones or television on the *Calypso*, Jean-Michel created his own fun. Much of that meant connecting with nature, a passion he shared with his father.

JEAN-MICHEL'S STORY:

My father pushed my late brother and me overboard when I was seven years old. We became instant scuba divers. He was unknown, but he was an inventor whose real job was to serve the French navy. We grew up with a dad who was an exceptional person, but we didn't realize that because he was unknown at the time. So we thought that what he was doing, everybody else was doing. What I think I owe him big time is to be an observer—to have a sense of enthusiasm as you discover things. And to literally understand the connections between things—animals, plants—which don't appear to have anything in common. I owe him all of that.

I remember at night when we went to bed (when he was home, often he was on his ship), he would read us the "The Law of the Jungle" by Kipling. I remember he would drag us out of our beds at midnight to show us the stars, to look at them and observe them and understand that in the Southern Hemisphere and in the Northern Hemisphere things are different. He would literally show our family the underwater world. We wanted to talk underwater. We would take the mouthpiece out of our mouths because my brother and I wanted to talk to each other. It was an ongoing yackety-yack in the silent world. That was all based on this enthusiasm for life that he had put into me. I feel extremely privileged because I saw it firsthand.

I experienced different cultures, races, religions, when I was ten, twelve, fifteen, traveling to different environments, in the Middle East, the Red Sea, the United States. After that, you understand tolerance. You understand the importance of diversity, which is synonymous with stability—that everything's connected, that if you disturb something, it may disturb many other things. I think if acquiring this enormous thirst for life, for discovery, happens before seventh grade, it will be with you forever.

In retrospect, I realized that going with my dad on his explorations was a fascinating thing. At the time, I did not know he was an unusual and talented person who brought the undersea world to millions. Then when I was eighteen, *The Silent World* came out. That was the first time I realized how much he had done. I've been very objective ever since, and I've been extremely grateful for this very privileged youth that I had.

HECTOR ELIZONDO

Actor

born: 1936

 **WHY HECTOR** ———————————————————○

Because Hector Elizondo is the man you've seen again and again playing the good guy, the crook, the chauffeur, the father, in his movies and Broadway shows. He's appeared in *The Princess Diaries* and *Tortilla Soup* and in many Arthur Miller plays.

Hector Elizondo grew up in the New York City neighborhood of West Harlem. He experienced a childhood rich in diverse cultures and learned the art of storytelling. Being chased by the bullies was also a common experience. His dad's advice helped him face his adversaries.

HECTOR'S STORY:

Age twelve was a turning point. After running home to my mother for the umpteenth time crying because the bullies chased me around the block again, my father said, "That's enough." Sitting me down in front of him, he said very clearly in Spanish, "Read my lips. We're not moving. Figure it out." That's the term he used:

"Figure it out." In other words: "You're a social animal. You're going to get your knees skinned. You're going to come back with a bloody nose sometimes. That's life. You can't be protected." The worst thing you can do is spoil a kid and tell them life is unfair. What we should teach kids above all else is what my father taught me: When you get knocked down, you get back up. No matter how clever you are, you're going to get hit. Surviving means learning how to get back up again.

Shortly after that particular encounter with my dad, he took me to the Police Athletic League, PAL, laced on the gloves, and started giving me boxing lessons. He taught me the old-fashioned way. I was not great at it, but I could see myself improving. I saw the results of my efforts. I still wasn't a fighter, but I felt better and started seriously working out. By the time I graduated from high school, I was an athlete.

WAYNE GRETZKY
Former Professional Hockey Player
born: 1961

❓ WHY WAYNE

Because Wayne Gretzky dominated the National Hockey League (NHL) for twenty seasons.

Because he helped Canada's Edmonton Oilers win four Stanley Cup Championships.

Because Gretzky rules as leader in goals and assists, and when he was traded to the Los Angeles Kings, he made hockey a major sports attraction in California for seven seasons.

Because of his greatness, when Gretzky retired in 1999 from the New York Rangers, his jersey number (99) was retired, too, a first in the NHL.

To become a sports icon takes hard work, lots of practice, and, of course, support from home. Wayne Gretzky credits his dad for doing everything he could to help Wayne pursue his passion. For those fans who have ever wondered why Gretzky always tucked in the right side of his jersey before each game, it was his dad's idea.

WAYNE'S STORY:

Not only was I six, I was a puny six, which meant the sweaters they had for the players looked like ballroom drapes on me. My sweater was so big it was constantly getting caught on my stick on my shooting side. One day my dad tucked the shooting side into my pants and it's been there ever since. Not that I'm superstitious or anything.

At the end of that year, I can remember coming home in my dad's car after the year-end banquet and crying.

"What's wrong?" my dad asked me.

"I didn't win a trophy," I cried. "Everybody won a trophy but me."

And my dad said something to me right then that I'll never forget.

"Wayne, keep practicing and one day you're gonna have so many trophies, we're not gonna have room for them all."

And he was right. Lots of kids as gifted as I was never had somebody like him to keep them on the right line. I don't know where I'd be without him, but I know it wouldn't be in the NHL.

ROALD DAHL   Writer
1916–1990

? WHY ROALD

Because his books are the first ones checked out of the library. Reading becomes an adventure with Ronald Dahl, who wrote *Charlie and the Chocolate*

Factory, The Twits, Matilda, James and the Giant Peach, Fantastic Mr. Fox, The BFG, and many more children's books.

Because he's on the kids' side—helping them with difficult and snooty adults, getting them in and out of bizarre situations, and making sure there are plenty of silly details to complete his hysterical stories.

Because it's Dahl's world—quirky and loved by all who read him again and again.

Roald Dahl was just three when his father and older sister died. Any memories of his father came from his early diary entries and from his mother's stories.

His Norwegian mother was the rock of the family, a voracious reader who instilled in Roald a love of books, especially exciting adventure stories. Typical of the times, at age nine, Roald was sent to boarding school—a difficult separation. He coped by writing to his mother faithfully and by employing a ritual that helped ease his loneliness.

ROALD'S STORY:

The first miserable homesick night at St. Peter's, when I curled up in bed and the lights were put out, I could think of nothing but our house at home and my mother and my sisters. Where were they? I asked myself. In which direction from where I was lying was Llandaff? I began to work it out and it wasn't difficult to do this because I had the Bristol Channel to help me. If I looked out of the dormitory window I could see the Channel itself, and the big city of Cardiff with Llandaff alongside it lay almost directly across the water but slightly to the north. Therefore if I turned towards the window I would be facing home. I wriggled round in my bed and faced my home and my family. From then on, during all the time I was at St. Peter's, I never went to sleep with my back to my family. Different beds in different dormitories required the working out of new directions, but the Bristol Channel was always my guide and I was always able to draw an imaginary line from my bed to our house over in Wales. Never once did I go to sleep looking away from my family. It was a great comfort to do this.

EARVIN "MAGIC" JOHNSON

Former Professional Basketball Player, Businessman

born: 1959

❓ WHY EARVIN

Because he's the pro-ball, All-Star, Olympic athlete who wowed fans by scoring when they thought he would pass and passing when they thought he would score.

Because as the point guard and forward for the Los Angeles Lakers for thirteen seasons, he helped his team bring home five NBA Championships, was voted MVP, and played in twelve All-Star tournaments.

Because after being infected with HIV, Magic retired from basketball and redefined himself as a businessman who focuses on revitalizing neglected communities and providing quality film and television entertainment to all.

Because he created the Magic Johnson Foundation, dedicated to serve the educational, health, and social needs of urban youth. That's why they call him Magic.

Due to his work schedule, Magic Johnson's dad couldn't always be at the junior high school games. But after each game, Magic always provided a play-by-play. When Lansing, Michigan, started noticing that they might have a real talent in town, his father's boss let him take time off to see his son score. Yes, both of his parents were proud, but Magic still had responsibilities at home—work still needed to be done.

EARVIN'S STORY:

My dad and I had a special bond that continues to this day. There's no question that basketball made us especially close. He didn't have much free time when I was a kid, but on Sunday afternoons we would sit together in the living room and watch NBA games on television. This was long before cable came along; there was only one game a week on TV, and that's what you watched.

My father's favorite player was Wilt Chamberlain, but we used to watch all the greats: Kareem Abdul-Jabbar and Oscar Robertson from Milwaukee, Bill Russell and John Havlicek from the Celtics, Elgin Baylor and Jerry West from the Lakers. During the games, my father would point out the subtleties of the pick-and-roll play, and explain the various defensive strategies.

When the game was over, Dad usually fell asleep on the couch. I'd run over to the Main Street courts at the schoolyard to practice some of the moves we had just seen. Sometimes Dad came with me, especially when a retooling at the plant gave him a few days off.

We'd play one-on-one, and he always beat me. He was really good, but he also played tough. Sometimes he'd hold me with one hand while he shot with the other. He poked me in the ribs and pushed me and grabbed me all over the court. I'd get mad, but he'd say, "No, that's not a foul!"—which only made me more frustrated, and pushed me to play harder, despite everything he was doing to harass me.

But that was the point. Dad was teaching me that I wouldn't always get the calls, that I had to play above the contact. He showed me different shots, like the two-handed set shot, which he had pretty well mastered. But above all he taught me how to be aggressive on the court: how to drive to the basket and take the charge; how to put up a shot as I was being hit. If they called the foul, great. And if they didn't, no problem.

He taught me to win against the odds, and never to quit. It was years before I was finally able to beat him one-on-one. But when I did, I knew I had really earned it.

Physically, I'm not the most gifted basketball player in the world. I've never been the fastest runner or the highest jumper. But thanks to my father, nobody will ever outsmart me on the court.

DAVE BARRY
Humor Columnist

born: 1947

? WHY DAVE

Because Dave Barry writes a newspaper column about ordinary events that makes readers laugh out loud at the absurdities of life.

Because Barry's Pulitzer Prize–winning humor column is syndicated nationally in over 500 newspapers.

Because he still wonders how that happened.

Because he has also written twenty-four books, including *Big Trouble*, which was made into a motion picture.

Are you naturally funny or did you inherit it? Probably a little of both. In Dave Barry's case, his environment helped him look at the zanier side of life. Humor was a survival tool for Dave in school, but he also employed it at home. Both parents had the comic gift. His father was more bookish in his approach to humor. His mother was a natural comedian who lived with a darker side. Both were Dave's biggest fans.

DAVE'S STORY:

My parents were smart, very literary, and very, very funny. My dad was a Presbyterian minister but not a conventional one. He didn't have a church. Instead, he worked for an inner-city organization in New York City called the New York City Mission Society. He was very involved in the Civil Rights Movement. He loved laughter and exposed me to lots of well-written humor. In particular, he loved Robert Benchley, P. G. Wodehouse, and people like that. Their books were always around, so he was a big influence.

My mom was the really crazy one. Literally. She struggled with mental illness, but when she was "on," she was probably the funniest person I ever knew. Her humor was very dark and edgy, not at all typical of suburban housewife humor of the 1950s. Life was sometimes very difficult and her humor reflected that. My idea of funny has always had a kind of "pushing the envelope" feel to it. I got that from my mother. After success hit, people would ask me who were my influences, and I always say, my sense of humor connects most directly with hers.

DANNY VILLANUEVA

Former Professional Football Player, Business Executive, Philanthropist

born: 1937

? WHY DANNY

Because he was the placekicker for the Los Angeles Rams from 1960 to 1964 and for the Dallas Cowboys from 1965 to 1967, and still holds several NFL kicking records.

Because during his playing years, Danny Villanueva worked part-time as a news director at KMEX-TV in Los Angeles. Moving up the corporate ladder, he became general manager and then president, turning KMEX into the most profitable Spanish-speaking television station in the United States.

Because his involvement with the Spanish-language television networks Univision and Telemundo changed the face of Spanish television.

Because Villanueva is passionate about young people and works with several nonprofits aimed at helping them stay in school.

Danny Villanueva's parents married at age fifteen and had sixteen children, two of whom were still-born and two who died while the family was moving from Mexico to California. Danny is the ninth of twelve surviving children. Even though he had to compete for attention, he always knew his mother was his best ally and biggest fan. Growing up in the border town of Calex-ico, Danny's life centered on church and school. Even with so many mouths to feed, his parents always set a place at the table for friends; one of them was the famous labor union leader Cesar Chavez.

His mom ruled the roost. She taught through example—a primary lesson being, success is not measured by what you have but by how much you give back.

DANNY'S STORY:

My mother was tough—her discipline, determination, and power held us together all those years. We owe much to that unschooled but wise woman who transformed herself, as she used to say, from an *indita* (a little Indian woman) into a formidable force in our lives.

Mom worked two jobs, as a domestic and at a tortilla factory. She and women from nearby border towns worked ten-hour days, sitting around a huge hot plate making tortillas and talking. My sisters told me those women were instrumental in changing my mother's ideas about life and family. In time, she took charge of the family and single-handedly changed my father, who had a hard time coping with the loss of their two babies.

Mom always loved music. On her way home from work, she used to stop at a little storefront church to listen to the singing. It was her way of forgetting about how hard work and life were. At first, she just listened, but then she joined in the singing, and before long she was part of the church. Then she dragged my dad in. He eventually became a preacher.

My brothers and sisters say I was always my

mother's project. Even after I was grown and playing in the NFL, she had me call every week. She worried about me. She complained about me. She called me *cabezón* (hard-headed) because I was stubborn.

Mom believed life offered windows of opportunity. "When they open, you must be prepared to step through them." Sometimes those opportunities last only seconds. Then you have to *meterle ganas* (go all out) to take advantage of them.

STEPHEN KING
Writer
born: 1947

? WHY STEPHEN

Because this king of storytelling knows how to scare, humor, and freak out his fans in ways that have them begging for more, whether it's through his page-turning novels, scary movies, or gripping short stories.

Because this author of the *Dark Tower* series, *Carrie, Cujo, Creepshow, Pet Sematary, Dreamcatcher, The Shining, The Green Mile, Stand by Me,* and *The Shawshank Redemption* believes he was born to do this job.

Because King's greatest gift is his imagination—a place so intriguing, millions buy his books and line up for his movies knowing they won't be disappointed.

Stephen King's dad left home when Stephen was two and never came back. Traveling from state to state and landing odd jobs to pay the bills was the way his mother supported her two young sons. Hard times did not discourage her—she provided for her family and was always there with an encouraging word. Stephen King had the habit of copying stories from comic books and giving them to his mother to read. After a time, she encouraged him to write his own stories because she believed her young son had talent. That's all he needed to hear. His mom gave him his first job and she was the first one to pay him for a job well done.

STEPHEN'S STORY:

I remember an immense feeling of *possibility* at the idea, as if I had been ushered into a vast building filled with closed doors and had been given leave to open any I liked. There were more doors than any one person could ever open in a lifetime, I thought (and still think).

I eventually wrote a story about four magic animals who rode around in an old car, helping out little kids. Their leader was a large white bunny named Mr. Rabbit Trick. He got to drive the car. The story was four pages long, laboriously printed in pencil. No one in it, so far as

I can remember, jumped from the roof of the Graymore Hotel. When I finished, I gave it to my mother, who sat down in the living room, put her pocketbook on the floor beside her, and read it all at once. I could tell she liked it—she laughed in all the right places—but I couldn't tell if that was because she liked me and wanted me to feel good or because it really *was* good.

"You didn't copy this one?" she asked when she had finished. I said no, I hadn't. She said it was good enough to be in a book. Nothing anyone has said to me since has made me feel any happier. I wrote four more stories about Mr. Rabbit Trick and his friends. She gave me a quarter apiece for them and sent them around to her four sisters, who pitied her a little, I think. *They* were all still married, after all; their men had stuck. It was true that Uncle Fred didn't have much sense of humor and was stubborn about keeping the top of his convertible up, it was also true that Uncle Oren drank quite a bit and had dark theories about how the Jews were running the world, but they were *there*. Ruth, on the other hand, had been left holding the baby when Don ran out. She wanted them to see that he was a talented baby, at least.

Four stories. A quarter apiece. That was the first buck I made in this business.

ARTHUR ASHE

Professional Tennis Player, Activist, Author

1943—1993

? WHY ARTHUR

Because Arthur Ashe, one of America's most distinguished tennis players, brought character and class to the courts.

Because he was the first African American to join the U.S. Davis Cup team and win a U.S tennis championship.

Because while he was ranked the number one tennis player in the world, he spoke out for players' rights, forming the Association of Tennis Professionals.

Because Ashe faced major health issues after retiring from tennis. In spite of two open-heart surgeries—one that infected him with HIV—he continued to speak out on race relations, apartheid, and AIDS until his death at age fifty.

Arthur Ashe discovered his love for tennis early. Growing up in Richmond, Virginia, he broke many color barriers, often being the only African American player on the court. He was a scrawny kid, but his tennis finesse ruled, landing him a tennis scholarship to UCLA.

His mother died when he was only six, yet her influence

was great. Later in life, whenever he was asked to speak about the morality in decisions one makes in life, his favorite refrain was, "Don't do anything you wouldn't tell your mother about." His father raised Arthur and his brother, impressing on them the importance of living an honest life.

ARTHUR'S STORY:

My father was a strong, dutiful, providing man. He lived and died semi-literate, but he owned his own home and held jobs that were important to him and to the people in the community where we lived. His love and his caring were real to me from that Sunday morning in 1950 when he sat on the bottom bunk bed between my brother Johnnie and me and told us between wrenching sobs that our mother had died during the night. From that time on, he was father and mother to us. And the lesson he taught above all was about reputation.

"What people think of you, Arthur Junior, your reputation, is all that counts." Or, as I heard from so many older people as I grew up, "A good name is worth more than diamonds and gold." What others think of me is important, and what I think of others is important. What else do I have to go by? Of course, I cannot make decisions based solely on what other people would think. There are moments when the individual must stand alone. Nevertheless, it is crucial to me that people think of me as honest and principled. . . .

One day, in Dallas, Texas, in 1973, I was playing in the singles final of a World Championship Tennis (WCT) tournament. My opponent was Stan Smith, a brilliant tennis player, but an even more impressive human being in his integrity. On one crucial point, I watched Smith storm forward, racing to intercept a ball about to bounce a second time on his side of the net. When the point was over, I was sure the ball had bounced twice before he hit it and that the point was mine. Smith said he had reached the ball in time. The umpire was baffled. The crowd was buzzing.

I called Smith up to the net.

"Stan, did you get to that ball?"

"I did. I got it."

I conceded the point. Later, after the match—which I lost—a reporter approached me. Was I so naïve? How could I have taken Smith's word on such an important point?

"Believe me," I assured him, "I am not a fool. I

wouldn't take just anybody's word for it. But if Stan Smith says he got to the ball, he got to it. I trust his character."

When I was not quite eighteen years old, I played a tournament in Wheeling, West Virginia, the Middle Atlantic Junior Championships. As happened much of the time when I was growing up, I was the only black kid in the tournament, at least in the under-eighteen age section. One night, some of the other kids trashed a cabin; they absolutely destroyed it. And then they decided to say that I was responsible, although I had nothing to do with it. The incident even got into the papers. As much as I denied and protested, those white boys would not change their story. . . .

When I reached Washington, where I was to play in another tournament, I telephoned him (my father). . . . As I was aware, he already knew about the incident. When he spoke, he was grim. But he had one question only.

"Arthur Junior, all I want to know is, were you mixed up in that mess?"

"No, Daddy, I wasn't."

He never asked about it again. He trusted me. With my father, my reputation was solid.

CHUCK LEAVELL

Rock and Roll Musician, Tree Farmer

born: 1952

? WHY CHUCK

Because when he's not playing keyboard for the Rolling Stones, he's a successful tree farmer in Georgia.

Because Chuck Leavell's talents have been tapped by Eric Clapton, the Black Crowes, George Harrison, the Indigo Girls, Blues Traveler, and many more.

Chuck Leavell has been called the sixth Rolling Stone for good reason. After twenty years, six tours, and ten CDs with Mick and the gang, Leavell knows a bit about playing keyboard for the legendary rock and roll band. He started playing folk music on a guitar, played tuba in junior high school, and was turned on to Ray Charles by his older sister, but it was his mother who jump-started his love of music. She'd play songs on the piano. Young Chuck listened and learned.

CHUCK'S STORY:

My parents influenced me in different ways. My mother instilled an appreciation that all men are created equal, that you get what you give and that you will be rewarded for the good things you do in life. My father taught me a lot about practicality. One thing he used to say that always stuck: "Son, you make your own luck in life." I think it's very true.

My mother played the piano for pure pleasure. Being the youngest of three siblings, oftentimes it was just me and Mom in the house, especially when I was real young, so the piano was my entertainment. I'd ask her to play, and I'd sit there watching, just fascinated. I loved watching her hands move across the keyboard. I would sit next to her and she would show me a few things. When she'd return to her housework, I would stay at the piano, picking out melodies or making them up. She always encouraged me, and at one point, both my parents said, "Why don't you take some lessons, Chuck?" I did, but I didn't have the discipline to stick with it. I'd rather be doing other things but always maintained my love and always sat down at our piano plunking out tunes.

LANCE ARMSTRONG

World, National, and Olympic Champion Cyclist

born: 1971

 ## WHY LANCE

Because nobody rides a bike better, longer, faster, than Lance Armstrong.

Because he brought home five (1999, 2000, 2001, 2002, 2003) Tour de France trophies.

Because the man with true grit found the toughest challenge in 1996, when he was diagnosed with testicular cancer that had spread to his lungs and brain.

Because he's not a quitter; he's a survivor who takes on challenges and likes to win.

Because he created the Lance Armstrong Foundation, which benefits cancer research and focuses on helping people manage and survive cancer.

With all odds against them, baby Lance and his seventeen-year-old mom were on their own. She was determined to give him everything he needed, with one unbending rule: "Make every obstacle an opportunity." This attitude saw Lance cross many finish lines, with Mom on the other side cheering him on. She also taught him independence and trusted him not to give her any problems. Lance held up his part of the deal.

From the very beginning, his mom believed in Lance's fortitude to be a champ.

LANCE'S STORY:

In Plano, Texas, if you weren't a football player, you didn't exist, and if you weren't upper middle class, you might as well not exist, either. I tried to play football. But I had no coordination. When it came to anything that involved a ball, in fact—I was no good.

I was determined to find something I could succeed at. When I was in fifth grade, my elementary school held a distance-running race. I told my mother the night before the race, "I'm going to be a champ." She just looked at me, and then went into her things and dug out a 1972 silver-dollar. "This is a good luck coin," she said. "Now remember, all you have to do is beat the clock." I won the race.

A few months later, I joined the local swim club. At first it was another way to seek acceptance with the other kids in the suburbs, who all swam laps at Los Rios Country Club, where their parents were members. On the first day of swim practice, I was so inept that I was put with the seven-year-olds. I looked around, and saw the younger sister of one of my friends. It was embarrassing.

I went from not being any good at football to not being any good at *swimming*.

But I tried. If I had to swim with the little kids to learn technique, then that's what I was willing to do. My mother gets emotional to this day when she remembers how I leaped headfirst into the water and flailed up and down the length of the pool, as if I was trying to splash all the water out of it. "You tried so *hard*," she says. I didn't swim in the worst group for long.

Swimming is a demanding sport for a 12-year-old, and the City of Plano Swim Club was particularly intense. I swam for a man named Chris MacCurdy, who remains one of the best coaches I ever worked with. Within a year, Chris transformed me; I was fourth in the state in the 1,500-meter freestyle. He trained our team seriously: we had workouts every morning from 5:30 to 7. Once I got a little older I began to ride my bike to practice, ten miles through the semi-dark early-morning streets. I would swim 4,000 meters of laps before school and go back for another two-hour workout in the afternoon—another 6,000 meters. That was six miles a day in the water, plus a 20-mile bike ride. My mother let me do it for two reasons: she didn't have the option of driving me herself because she worked, and she knew that I needed to channel my temperament.

CHAPTER 3

DEFINING TIMES

Experiences That Shape the Man

Experience is not what happens to a man; it is what a man does with what happens to him.

—ALDOUS HUXLEY

You remember the day your life changed. You recall the pit in your stomach when you realized life isn't fair. And you still revel in the feeling you had when she finally smiled back and actually talked to you. These are first-timers. Moments that you never saw coming. Moments you'll never forget. Some are great, some are painful, and some turn you into a sentimental slob. It's what they call life and there's no avoiding it. Open your mind. Take in the moments. Experience what it really feels like to live outside the lines.

Life is constantly throwing us curveballs. We can

strike out and try again or give it our best shot and maybe even hit a home run. The men in this chapter share their own personal defining moments that left imprints on their memories and often changed the way they thought about the world. For photographer Ansel Adams, the destructive force of the San Francisco earthquake in 1906 shaped his life. Martin Luther King, Jr., grew up with racial hatred and learned early what it felt like to be judged by the color of one's skin. And Coach Dean Smith remembered how hopeless he felt after his best friend died from polio.

Times have changed a lot since these three men were boys. Advancements in tolerance and technology have helped your generation deal with many of the obstacles they faced. But progress brings new obstacles. Issues you and your friends face now weren't even on the radar screen when Adams, King, and Smith were boys.

This is your story now. Your defining moments will differ in some ways, yet there's still a good chance your emotions and reactions will be very similar to those of the men you read about. See what you have in common with them. Perhaps there is a lesson or a moment of truth that will help you to overcome your obstacles.

Their defining moments might offer knowledge about life and its many dimensions. Who knows, it might even help you hit that curveball aimed right at you.

Speak your mind, form an opinion, and you'll be equipped to take on life's biggest challenges, just as these men did.

EARVIN "MAGIC" JOHNSON

Former Professional Basketball Player, Businessman

born: 1959

 WHY EARVIN

Because he's the pro-ball, All-Star, Olympic athlete who wowed fans by scoring when they thought he would pass and passing when they thought he would score.

Because as the point guard and forward for the Los Angeles Lakers for thirteen seasons, he helped his team bring home five NBA Championships, was voted MVP, and played in twelve All-Star tournaments.

Because after being infected with HIV, Magic retired from basketball and redefined himself as a businessman who focuses on revitalizing neglected communities and providing quality film and television entertainment to all.

Because he created the Magic Johnson Foundation, dedicated to serve the educational, health, and social needs of urban youth. That's why they call him Magic.

Magic Johnson learned early that nothing lasts forever when one of his best friends died suddenly. He couldn't believe it. They had such big plans. There was basketball to play and girls to date. This painful life lesson taught Magic Johnson about courage.

EARVIN'S STORY:

A lot of who I am today has to do with the people I was close to when I was growing up. There were my parents, of course, and my family, and Jim and Greta Dart. But in my teenage years it was my friends who seemed to matter most.

What my pal Reggie Chastine lacked in height, he more than made up in self-confidence. He had so much faith in his own abilities that it was almost as if he could peel off some of his extra self-assurance and hand it over to me.

I definitely needed it. This might sound strange, given everything that happened to me later, but when I started high school I was full of doubts about just how good I really was. Would I be able to keep up with guys on other teams who could run right past me and jump right over me? Sure, I was a big deal in Lansing, but Lansing was nothing. What would happen when we played some of those really strong teams from Detroit?

"Are you kidding?" Reggie would say. "You're going all the way, man. I don't care where you're from. I just know *where* you're going, and that's the NBA."

He was a year ahead of me at Everett, but we did

everything together. He would pick me up every morning so we could drive to school together. After class, we'd practice together with the team. During the final minutes of a game, when we were blowing out the other team and the subs had come in, the two of us would sit together on the bench. We'd pretend to watch the game, but we were actually scanning the crowd, looking for pretty girls. Sometimes Reggie would pick out a couple of girls who were sitting together. He'd write them a note and the team manager would bring it over, asking them to wait for us after the game. Sometimes they did. Once, after a game in Jackson, Reggie met a girl he really liked. Before long, he was driving to Jackson to see her on weekends.

When Reggie graduated, he won a basketball scholarship to Eastern Michigan University. That summer I often drove with him to Jackson, where I had a girlfriend, too. I forgot why, but just before one of these trips I had to cancel out at the last minute. Reggie promised to call when he got there. When I didn't hear from him, I figured something had come up.

Early the next morning I got a call from Reggie's younger brother. He told me that the night before, Reggie's car had been hit by a drunk driver who had run a stop sign. Reggie, my best friend, had been killed instantly.

No! No! No! As soon as I hung up the phone, I left my house and started running. I ran for hours, it seemed, the tears streaming down my face. I didn't know where I was headed, but I just kept going. I couldn't stop, didn't want to stop. If I stopped running, that would make it true.

I couldn't believe that Reggie's life was over just like that. He had plans. He had a *future!* I was going to watch him play in college. And Reggie was going to come back to see us at Everett.

In his senior year we had reached the semifinals. And this season, which was starting in just a few weeks, we had a good chance to go all the way, to win the state championship. "I know you guys can take it," Reggie had told us when he graduated. "And I'll be back to cheer you on."

This was my first experience with death, and it was devastating. When you're young, and you lose somebody your own age, it's a shock you never forget. The whole community was stunned. Everybody loved Reggie, this scrappy little fighter who not only made the team, but became a starter. He had so much heart. He feared nobody. And he taught me about courage when I really needed to learn it.

GREG LOUGANIS
Olympic and World Champion Diver

born: 1960

❓ WHY GREG

Because he's considered the world's greatest diver. Greg Louganis was the first person in fifty-six years to win Olympic gold medals in both springboard and platform events. He was also the first to win the gold in two consecutive Olympics.

Because he's a six-time world champion and has held forty-seven national championships.

Because he came home from the 1988 Olympics with the Maxwell House/U.S. Olympic Committee Spirit Award, given to athletes who demonstrate courage and contribute significantly to their sport.

Because Louganis has HIV and became a valiant spokesperson for gay rights and AIDS victims after the release of his autobiography, *Breaking the Surface*.

At twelve years old, Greg Louganis's life bottomed out. He was depressed, on drugs, and had no real friends. Greg lashed out and actually pushed his mother across the room, an act that forced his parents to send him to juvenile hall in hopes of straightening him out. The flood-gates finally opened and Greg started expressing anger and depression to his parents. He needed to learn more about his birth parents. Not knowing haunted him. Fortunately, Greg's adoptive parents were willing to help him with that chapter of his life. A defining moment occurred when he learned the truth about his birth parents.

GREG'S STORY:

We met again with the counselor the next day, and I started talking. One of the things that came out during the counseling session was that I wanted to find out more about my natural parents. My parents agreed that I could go to the adoption agency and ask whatever questions I wanted to about my natural parents.

My parents also talked privately with the counselor and arranged the terms under which I could be released. I was allowed to go home if I agreed to go straight home from school for the rest of the school year, to help my mother around the house with whatever needed to be done, and to not hang out with my friends.

During the six months after my stay in juvenile hall, my mother and I got much closer. I know she was happy about the change, because she told me that I'd gone back to being her "sweet, lovable, handsome boy."

Every day after school, I'd come home and we'd sit at the kitchen table and talk for an hour or so. Sometimes we talked about diving. Sometimes we talked about school. Our relationship really turned around. She didn't judge me. She made me feel it was okay to feel and think whatever I was thinking or feeling at the time.

As promised, after I got out of juvenile hall, we made a trip to the adoption agency that had handled my case. I found out what my biological dad looked like and that he was interested in sports. I didn't find out much more about my mother than I already knew, except that she was living in San Diego. I didn't know where my father was. My father had apparently wanted to keep me, and his parents wanted to raise me as his brother. That alone was enough to convince me that my natural parents cared about me. That's what I needed to hear the most: that I was wanted. But I also found out that my natural mother didn't want me raised by my father's family because, the adoption agency said, she wanted me to have more opportunities in life than they could offer.

It was comforting to know that thought went into the decision to put me up for adoption. I had always assumed that my biological parents didn't love me. There were so many blank spots in the story, and I had chosen to fill them in as negatively as I could imagine, a pattern I repeated often in my life. I assumed that my biological parents had simply wanted to unload me. I never thought that giving me up might have been a difficult decision for them.

At that point my curiosity was satisfied. I knew I had been loved by my natural parents, and I realized that the Louganises *were* my family. My natural parents may have been the two fifteen-year-olds who had me, but Peter and Frances Louganis would always be my real parents. That realization really helped turn things around for me. But the emotional damage had already been done, and I've struggled throughout my life with trusting whether anyone genuinely cared for me.

JAMES CAMERON

Film Director, Producer, Writer

born: 1954

? WHY JAMES

Because he's the special-effects king, creator, and mastermind behind the action films *Terminator, Aliens, True Lies, The Abyss,* and *Titanic.*

Because James Cameron wowed the world with *Titanic*, which garnered eleven Academy Awards and earned more money than any other movie in the history of filmmaking.

James Cameron was born to lead. He loved science fiction and spent his childhood examining and questioning how everything worked. Even as a young boy, Cameron had a knack for convincing friends to experiment and try new things. Positive results encouraged him to push the envelope further, to experiment more, which all added up to be defining moments for the future filmmaker. The power of persuasion honed in childhood would be utilized on his movie sets later on.

JAMES'S STORY:

I was a curious kid about how things worked, from the natural world to biology to physics. I wanted to know about the planets and stars and that sort of thing. My parents always knew I'd be happy if they bought me a microscope, a chemistry set, or a telescope that I could assemble myself.

It's funny, but I remember feeling pretty secure with who I was at a very young age, by seven or eight. The way I spent my time, exploring and making stuff, didn't seem odd to me at all. It was only later on, when I entered high school, that my peers started to wonder about me, because by then they knew I was looking at the world through a different lens than they were.

I had my own group of friends. Frankly, I hung out with the misfits of the school. Those kids who were either creative and artistic or oriented to writing or even politics. I never did gravitate toward the mainstream activities at my high school.

I was always comfortable in my own head. It was a fun place to be, imagining other worlds and making up stories. I was that kid who always got the other kids in the neighborhood to build a fort, but not just any fort. If we were pretending to be members of the Iroquois tribe, then it was important we build an Iroquois long-house, using only the hand tools they used. I remember a group of us out in the woods stripping bark off trees with knives and hatchets and one kid pulling out a claw hammer to use, but I told him he couldn't use it because the Iroquois didn't have claw hammers back then. That was the time we were running around in our underwear because we had to be real Indians. The only problem was, we all got poison ivy and had to go to the hospital. So that project wasn't exactly successful. But there was always some project that was so critically important to do and I always seemed to be able to persuade my friends to do it.

Not much has changed. Instead of saying, "Okay, guys, let's build a fort," now I say, "Let's make a movie." It's only been recently that I've been able to see the link between the way I related as a kid to the way I relate now. It's innate. It's just who I am.

COLIN POWELL

**Secretary of State,
G. W. Bush Administration**

born: 1937

? WHY COLIN

Because he represents what an American can accomplish in this great land of opportunity. After a stellar career in the army, the son of Jamaican immigrants served as the twelfth chairman of the Joint Chiefs of Staff from 1989 to 1993, the highest military position in the Department of Defense. During his chairmanship, Powell oversaw operations in the Persian Gulf War.

Because in 2001, this decorated hero became secretary of state under the George W. Bush administration. Secretary Colin Powell is a symbol of honor.

Like many kids, Colin Powell sometimes got mixed up with the wrong crowd. He remembered one particular incident that turned into a defining moment by teaching him how to face problems head on.

COLIN'S STORY:

I was a believer, but no saint. One summer, in the early fifties, Father Weeden selected me, the son of two pillars of St. Margaret's, to go to a church camp near Peekskill. Once there, I promptly fell into bad company. One night, my newfound friends and I snuck out to buy beer. We hid it in the toilet tank to cool, but our cache was quickly discovered. The priest in charge summoned all campers to the meeting hall. He did not threaten or berate us. Instead, he asked who was ready to accept responsibility. Who would own up like a man? We could probably have gotten away with our transgression by saying nothing. But his words struck me. I stood up. "Father, I did it," I said. When they heard me, two more budding hoodlums rose up and also confessed.

We were put on the next train back to New York. Word of our sinning preceded us. I dragged myself up Westchester Avenue and turned right onto Kelly Street like a felon mounting the gallows. As I reached number 952, there was Mom, her usually placid face twisted into a menacing scowl. When she finished laying into me, Pop began. Just about when I thought I was eternally damned, Father Weeden telephoned. Yes, the boys had behaved badly, he said. "But your Colin stood up and took responsibility. And his example spurred the other boys to admit their guilt." My parents beamed. From juvenile delinquent, I had been catapulted to hero. Something from that boyhood experience, the rewards of honesty, hit home and stayed.

TUPAC SHAKUR

Musician, Poet

1971–1996

 WHY TUPAC

Because 2Pac still rules. Even after his death from a gunshot wound at age twenty-five, the stories of heartbreak, ambition, and passion told in the music of this controversial and introspective street poet still appeal to all races.

Tupac Shakur knew all about curveballs. He grew up tough in a neighborhood complicated by gangs. But his tough image was not always what it seemed. Sometimes he felt vulnerable and lonely. Sometimes he just needed someone to listen to him. His poem says it all.

SOMETIMES I CRY

Sometimes when I'm alone
I cry because I'm on my own
The tears I cry R bitter and warm
They flow with life but take no form
I cry because my heart is torn
and I find it difficult 2 carry on
If I had an ear 2 confide in
I would cry among my treasured friends
But who do u know that stops that long
to help another carry on
The world moves fast and it would rather pass u by
than 2 stop and c what makes u cry
It's so painful and sad sometimes I cry
and no one cares about why.

CHARLES CHAMPLIN

Writer, Former Film Critic and Talk-Show Host

born: 1926

? WHY CHARLES

Because he knows celebrities up close and personal. As a reporter for *Time* and *Life* magazines, Charles Champlin wrote about the emerging arts culture in America and abroad.

Because while living in London, he suggested to *Time* magazine that they run a story about a little-known band called the Beatles. *Time* magazine passed on the request, and a year later, the Beatles invaded America.

Because as the author of over ten books, Champlin has written about the careers of his friends Alfred Hitchcock, George Lucas, John Frankenheimer, and Woody Allen.

Because he was the film critic and arts editor for the *Los Angeles Times* for three decades, and was the host of *Champlin on Film,* a TV series on Bravo, featuring guests such as Dustin Hoffman, Danny Glover, Tom Hanks, Hugh Grant, and Jodie Foster.

A most defining time came for Charles Champlin when his father left home. Justifying his father's whereabouts made him uncomfortable, which was one reason why he turned inward, seeking the comfort of books and writing. Living in Hammondsport, a lakeside town in upper New York State, Champlin's mother counted on her son's good behavior. He did not disappoint.

CHARLES'S STORY:

My mother had employed Fred and Jack and Joe to tend the furnace and do the heavy chores because from almost the earliest days I can remember we were a fatherless household. Marriages don't fall apart tidily, and my father had not so much disappeared as faded out like the end of a movie scene. I find it almost impossible to conjure up memories of him in the Hammondsport house. My parents separated permanently when I was about six and were divorced when I was nine.

A half-century later divorce is so frequent at every level of society and in every state of the Union that it is difficult to convey the impact—in a small town in the thirties—of having one's parents divorce.

I never felt the guilt that children are supposed to feel. I was certain that my brother and I were not responsible for the break-up of the marriage. Aside from a little noise early on Sunday mornings, we were fairly orderly children, not given to tantrums, running away or setting things on fire. The worst that could be said of us was that our presence had failed to hold the marriage together, as children are alleged to do. But at the time it seemed to me that guilt was all I was spared. I felt more than a little bit ashamed, as if something had happened in my family that did not happen in nice families and was unacceptable. . . .

Back in Hammondsport, and even before the formal separation, I had been teased about my absent father.

"When's your father coming home, Charles?" a particularly malevolent older boy asked me every time he saw me.

"He's away on business a lot," I remember saying, trying not to let him know that I knew or suspected the real truth, or that he had hit me where it hurt a lot. Small-town children do not have a monopoly on small cruelties, but they perform them very well.

One night when I was nine and reading in bed (an early habit) my mother came upstairs with a copy of the Corning *Leader* and said we might read it together—an odd and unprecedented suggestion. She quickly found her way to a small boxed item on an inside page, slugged "Special to the *Leader*." It reported that she had been granted a divorce from my father. It was an awkward and painful moment for both of us and I thought it was a curious and oblique way to break the news, but in those circumstances no way is better or worse than another. . . .

The most uncomfortable part of the evening my mother brought me the news of the divorce was that I had very little idea how to comfort her or what to begin to say to her. I would now have to be the man of the house, she said, a theme that was repeated by two grandmothers and assorted aunts and uncles over the next several weeks. It was like dialogue from a not very good film but I went along because I agreed and because I didn't have much choice. In my darkest moments I felt as if I were being trapped into inescapable good behavior and a joyless early maturity. This was not entirely true. Yet I think that being raised by our mother alone, in circumstances that were difficult for her socially as well as economically, had the effect of foreshortening childhood for both my brother and me.

I imagine that most children speculate sooner or later on how they and their lives might have been different if their parents had not been divorced. I've fantasized about it a lot over the years. With my father around, I might have been more of a hand with tools and practical matters; I might have been a chemist, might have gone to a different college, might have ended up in the wine business. I might have been less introspective and more extroverted in my early years, might have spent fewer of my childhood and adolescent hours by myself, reading, and I might not have become a writer. And, then again, given the particular patchwork of genes I have within me, I might have ended up much as I have. I can't imagine being totally happy except as a writer.

GLEN BALLARD
Songwriter, Producer

born: 1953

WHY GLEN

Because this five-time Grammy Award winner cowrote and produced Alanis Morissette's album *Jagged Little Pill*.

Because Glen Ballard has written and produced songs for Michael Jackson, Shelby Lynne, Van Halen, Dave Matthews Band, Aerosmith, and many others.

Because as the music industry's most sought-after writer and producer, Ballard's number one goal is helping musicians realize their artistic vision.

Growing up in Natchez, Mississippi, Glen Ballard was influenced by certain people and teachers, but it was music—blues, jazz, and soul—and the people playing it that influenced him the most. From a very early age, Ballard was able to decode the piano and just play songs. His defining time came during exposure to musicians from the area. They taught him how to listen and how to compose his own work.

GLEN'S STORY:

I think Natchez was a relatively idyllic setting, but I certainly felt the pull of the world at large. I think I innately knew that I would not be living my life in Mississippi, and I had no idea, when I became an adult, how I was going to sort of move out of there or achieve some kind of escape velocity from that place in the world. So while it was a positive time, I also knew I wanted more.

I think the music that I was surrounded by was so varied and was the greatest influence because I was hearing a lot of great local music. I learned how to play the guitar from an older gentleman who played the blues. His grandfather was a slave and he really knew about the blues. He taught me how to tune the guitar and gave me this real sense of connection to the roots of blues in Mississippi. Combine that with the incredible local music I was hearing from artists out of New Orleans and Memphis and the Beatles from England and I knew there was so much to learn. There were things happening in the culture at large, but there was the local radio station that would play local artists. Unfortunately, that concept is just a thing of the past now. You could turn on a radio and hear something you couldn't hear anywhere else in the country, especially around New Orleans. Spending a lot of time there and being around people who were passionate about music, not as a business, but just as something that they had to express, was an enormously rich influence. So I always thought of music as being something that was part of the whole culture. I was absorbed by it.

NELSON MANDELA
Former President of South Africa
born: 1918

? WHY NELSON

Because Nelson Mandela fought for the freedom of South African blacks by devoting his life to fighting apartheid (the practice of separating people based on their race). His beliefs caused him to spend twenty-seven years in jail.

Because upon his release, he was recognized as an international hero and elected president of South Africa.

Because his commitment to the freedom of black South Africans earned him the Nobel Peace Prize.

Nelson Mandela was a member of the Thembu tribe, a group of the Xhosa nation in South Africa. His father was a leader in the tribe and Mandela was groomed to follow in his footsteps. After his father's death when Nelson was just nine years old, he came under the guidance of a new guardian, another leader in the tribe. For the next several years, he was groomed for leadership with a solid education from the best schools.

In the Thembu tribe, a boy's rite of passage into manhood takes place at age sixteen, during the customary ritual of circumcision. For Nelson Mandela, this ceremony was the most defining moment of his youth.

NELSON'S STORY:

When I was sixteen, the regent decided that it was time that I became a man. In Xhosa tradition, this is achieved through one means only: circumcision. In my tradition, an uncircumcised male cannot be heir to his father's wealth, cannot marry or officiate in tribal rituals. An uncircumcised Xhosa man is a contradiction in terms, for he is not considered a man at all, but a boy. For the Xhosa people, circumcision represents the formal incorporation of males into society. It is not just a surgical procedure, but a lengthy and elaborate ritual in preparation for manhood. As a Xhosa, I count my years as a man from the date of my circumcision.

The traditional ceremony of the circumcision school was arranged principally for Justice—the rest of us, twenty-six in all, were there mainly to keep him company. Early in the new year, we journeyed to two grass huts in a secluded valley on the banks of the Mbashe River, known as Tyhalarha, the traditional place of circumcision for Thembu kings. The huts were seclusion lodges, where we were to live isolated from society. It was a sacred time; I felt happy and fulfilled taking part in my people's customs and ready to make the transition from boyhood to manhood. . . .

At dawn, when the stars were still in the sky, we began our preparations. We were escorted to the river to bathe in its cold waters, a ritual that signified our purification before the ceremony. The ceremony was at midday, and we were commanded to stand in a row in a clearing some distance from the river where a crowd of parents and relatives, including the regent, as well as a handful of chiefs and counselors, had gathered. We were clad only in our blankets, and as the ceremony began, with drums pounding, we were ordered to sit on a blanket on the ground with our legs spread out in front of us. I was tense and anxious, uncertain of how I would react when the critical moment came. Flinching or crying out was a sign of weakness and stigmatized one's manhood. I was determined not to disgrace myself, the group, or my guardian. Circumcision is a trial of bravery and stoicism; no anesthetic is used; a man must suffer in silence.

To the right, out of the corner of my eye, I could see a thin elderly man emerge from a tent and kneel in front of the first boy. There was excitement in the crowd, and I shuddered slightly knowing that the ritual was about to begin. The old man was a famous *ingcibi*, a circumcision expert, from Gcalekaland, who would use his assegai to change us from boys to men with a single blow.

Suddenly, I heard the first boy cry out, *"Ndiyindoda!"* (I am a man!), which we were trained to say in the moment of circumcision. Seconds later, I heard Justice's strangled voice pronounce the same phrase. There were now two boys before the *ingcibi* reached me, and my mind must have gone blank because before I knew it, the old man was kneeling in front of me. I looked directly into his eyes. He was pale, and though the day was cold, his face was shining with perspiration. His hands moved so fast they seemed to be controlled by an otherworldly force. Without a word, he took my foreskin, pulled it forward, and then, in a single motion, brought down his assegai. I felt as if fire was shooting through my veins; the pain was so intense that I buried my chin into my chest. Many seconds seemed to pass before I remembered the cry, and then I recovered and called out, *"Ndiyindoda!"*

I looked down and saw a perfect cut, clean and round like a ring. But I felt ashamed because the other boys seemed much stronger and braver than I had been; they had called out more promptly than I had. I was distressed that I had been disabled, however briefly, by the pain, and I did my best to hide my agony. A boy may cry; a man conceals his pain.

DEAN SMITH

Former College Basketball Coach

born: 1931

? WHY DEAN

Because as the former head coach for the University of North Carolina, Dean Smith won more games than any other coach in basketball history.

Because for thirty-six years, Smith led his team to eleven Final Fours, two national titles, and thirteen ACC Tournament Championships.

Because he is recognized as one of the great minds of basketball, he was respected by his players (96 percent graduated during his tenure), and he managed to win consistently.

Because he taught Michael Jordan how to be a champ.

The times you live in often shape the man you will become. When Dean Smith was growing up in the '30s and '40s, polio was epidemic and World War II was being waged overseas. Both events invaded his carefree life in Kansas. Dean's idol, Jack Snow, who played basketball on his father's team, was killed fighting for our country. Then his close friend Shad Woodruff died of polio. Dean Smith's life would be changed forever. He had lost his comfort zone.

DEAN'S STORY:

Not long afterwards, a larger event in our lives reminded me that there were more serious matters than the outcome of a baseball game. One of my friends in those years was a boy named Shad Woodruff, a housepainter's son who was just about the best athlete in town. He was the leading dash man on our ninth-grade track team, a top scorer on the basketball team, our baseball center fielder, and my favorite receiver on the football field. He was popular too, an open-natured young man who was impossible to dislike, and his entire family was the same way. His mother, whom we called Boots, was warm and sincere, and kids naturally gravitated to her house.

On the July 4 weekend of the summer of 1945, Shad and I played in an American Legion baseball double-header. Afterwards he said he didn't feel too good and decided to go home. By the time he got there, he was so ill he had to be taken to the hospital. The diagnosis was bulbar polio. I hurried to the hospital and stood outside his room, but nobody would let me in to see him, because polio was thought to be so contagious. It was before the Salk vaccine, and polio was epidemic. A lot of communities had quarantines in effect, and we heard stories of kids being confined to their homes and backyards for whole summers. But I never expected it to visit Emporia like this. Shad and I had shared the same water bucket on the Fourth.

I stood vigil outside Shad's room for most of the day and into the night. Four days later he died. It shattered all of us. Despite the realities of the war, it was the first time I had lost someone truly close to me, my own age, and I struggled to understand it. I found it so impossible to grasp that I spent days leafing through clippings and pictures of Shad. Finally, I took a pair of scissors and began to trim the newspaper clippings into neat squares and paste them into a book. I cut and pasted until I had created an entire album of Shad. I carried the album over to the Woodruffs' and gave the book to Shad's parents. We stayed in touch for the rest of their lives, until they died fifteen or so years ago.

To me, that period was very much about loss. Jack Snow and Shad Woodruff seemed part of the same ungraspable sorrow. One day they were vivid presences in our lives, and the next, they were photographs in an album. I think anyone who grew up during World War II, in that era of victory gardens and polio epidemics and young soldiers poised on the doorstep, must remember their childhoods as bittersweet.

MARTIN LUTHER KING, JR. 1929–1968

Civil Rights Leader, Pastor

? WHY MARTIN

Because he was the leader of America's greatest non-violent movement for justice, equality, and peace.

Because Martin Luther King, Jr., had a dream that people would not be judged by the color of their skin but by the content of their character.

Because through his selfless devotion, he taught others to celebrate human worth by offering black people and the poor hope and a sense of dignity.

Because he received the Nobel Peace Prize in 1964 at the age of thirty-five, the youngest man, second American, and third African American to be so honored.

Because a national holiday is observed in honor of his January 15 birthday. Martin Luther King, Jr., was assassinated because of his beliefs.

Understanding abstract concepts is one of life's first challenges. Martin Luther King's grandmother's death when he was quite young had a profound effect and made him question the concept of immortality. His first experience with racism also made a huge impact on young Martin. Not being allowed to play with someone because of his skin color did not make sense to him. This experience would pave the way for Martin Luther King to become committed to changing prevailing attitudes about race.

MARTIN'S STORY:

Two incidents happened in my late childhood and early adolescence that had a tremendous effect on my development. The first was the death of my grandmother. She was very dear to each of us, but especially to me. I sometimes think I was her favorite grandchild. I was particularly hurt by her death mainly because of the extreme love I had for her. She assisted greatly in raising all of us. It was after this incident that for the first time I talked at any length on the doctrine of immortality. My parents attempted to explain it to me, and I was assured that somehow my grandmother still lived. I guess this is why today I am such a strong believer in personal immortality.

The second incident happened when I was about six years of age. From the age of three I had a white playmate who was about my age. We always felt free to play our childhood games together. He did not live in our community, but he was usually around every day; his father owned a store across the street from our home. At the age of six we both entered school—separate schools, of course. I remember how our friendship began to break as soon as we entered school; this was not my desire but his. The climax came when he told me one day that his father had demanded that he would play with me no more. I never will forget what a great shock this was to me. I immediately asked my parents about the motive behind such a statement.

We were at the dinner table when the situation was discussed, and here for the first time I was made aware of the existence of a race problem. I had never been conscious of it before. As my parents discussed some of the tragedies that had resulted from this problem and some of the insults they themselves had confronted on account of it, I was greatly shocked, and from that moment on I was determined to hate every white person. As I grew older and older this feeling continued to grow.

My parents would always tell me that I should not hate the white man, but that it was my duty as a Christian to love him. The question arose in my mind: How could I love a race of people who hated me and who had been responsible for breaking me up with one of my best childhood friends? This was a great question in my mind for a number of years.

STEPHEN KING

Writer

born: 1947

 WHY STEPHEN

Because this king of storytelling knows how to scare, humor, and freak out his fans in ways that have them begging for more, whether it's through his page-turning novels, scary movies, or gripping short stories.

Because this author of the *Dark Tower* series, *Carrie*, *Cujo*, *Creepshow*, *Pet Sematary*, *Dreamcatcher*, *The Shining*, *The Green Mile*, *Stand by Me*, and *The Shaw-shank Redemption* believes he was born to do this job.

Because King's greatest gift is his imagination—a place so intriguing, millions buy his books and line up for his movies knowing they won't be disappointed.

As a kid, Stephen King knew what it was like to be sick. His interest in writing was born because he spent so much time in bed. Most of first grade was missed due to strep throat, measles, and severe ear infections, so he spent his time reading everything from comic books to Jack London's animal tales. One of the first stories he wrote was titled "Happy Stamps" inspired by his mother's interest in purchasing household items with S & H Green Stamps. In King's day, S & H Green Stamps were given out like coupons. People collected booklets full. He submitted the piece to *Alfred Hitchcock's Mystery Magazine* (AHMM). It came back with a note that simply said, "Don't staple manuscripts." Informing King to use paper clips instead, this first of many rejection slips quietly encouraged Stephen King to keep on writing.

STEPHEN'S STORY:

My room in our Durham house was upstairs, under the eaves. At night I could lie in bed beneath one of these eaves—if I sat up suddenly, I was apt to whack my head a good one—and read by the light of a gooseneck lamp that put an amusing boa constrictor of shadow on the ceiling. Sometimes the house was quiet except for the whoosh of the furnace and the patter of rats in the attic; sometimes my grandmother would spend an hour or so around midnight yelling for someone to check Dick, a horse she'd had in her day as a schoolteacher, who was at least forty years dead. I had a desk beneath the room's other eave, my old Royal typewriter, and a hundred or so paperback books, mostly science fiction, which I lined up along the baseboard. On my bureau was a Bible won for memorizing verses in Methodist Youth Fellowship and a Webcor phonograph with an automatic changer and a turntable covered in soft green velvet. On it I played my records, mostly 45s by Elvis, Chuck Berry, Freddy Cannon and Fats Domino. I liked Fats; he knew how to rock, and you could tell he was having fun.

When I got the rejection slip from AHMM, I pounded a nail into the wall above the Webcor, wrote "Happy Stamps" on the rejection slip, and poked it onto the nail. Then I sat on my bed and listened to Fats sing "I'm Ready." I felt pretty good actually. When you're still too young to shave, optimism is a perfectly legitimate response to failure.

By the time I was fourteen (and shaving twice a week whether I needed to or not) the nail in my wall would no longer support the weight of the rejection slips impaled upon it. I replaced the nail with a spike and went on writing. By the time I was sixteen I'd begun to get rejection slips with handwritten notes a little more encouraging than the advice to stop using staples and start using paperclips. The first of these hopeful notes was from Algis Budry, then the editor of *Fantasy and Science Fiction,* who read a story of mine called "The Night of the Tiger" (the inspiration was, I think, an episode of *The Fugitive* in which Dr. Richard Kimble worked as an attendant cleaning out cages in a zoo or circus) and wrote: "This is good. Not for us, but good. You have talent. Submit again."

Those four brief sentences, scribbled by a fountain pen that left big ragged blotches in its wake, brightened the dismal winter of my sixteenth year. Ten years or so later, after I sold a couple of novels, I discovered "The Night of the Tiger" in a box of old manuscripts and thought it was still a perfectly respectable tale, albeit one obviously written by a guy who had only begun to learn his chops. I rewrote it and on a whim resubmitted it to F&SF. This time they bought it. One thing I've noticed is that when you have a little success, magazines are a lot less apt to use that phrase, "Not for us."

ERNIE BARNES
Artist, Former Professional Football Player
born: 1938

❓ WHY ERNIE

Because Ernie Barnes played center, tackle, and guard for the Baltimore Colts, the San Diego Chargers, and the Denver Broncos.

Because he has always looked at life as an artist, even when he was playing professional football. Known today as one of America's most respected contemporary figurative painters, Ernie Barnes has combined his two passions by depicting athletic events in his art.

Because Barnes chose to become a full-time artist in 1965, when the owner of the New York Jets commissioned him to do a series of paintings for more money than he had ever earned in football.

During freshman year of high school in Durham, North Carolina, playing sports wasn't even on the radar screen for Ernie Barnes. Overweight and extremely introverted, he preferred drawing to tough physical workouts. His defining moment came when a teacher urged him to beef up and play football.

ERNIE'S STORY:

The year I entered the ninth grade, I was eligible for varsity, but I didn't go out for the team voluntarily—not for the varsity team at Hillside High School. These were mature brutes. Some of them were over six-feet and looked to be in their late twenties. Hillside High was known throughout the state for excellence in every sport.

So I went back to saying, "I want to, but my mother won't let me." My mother had been given specific instructions (from me) to just say "no" to anyone asking about me playing football. I felt it was firmly understood. I felt secure from recruitment.

My habit of hiding out in less-traveled areas of the school didn't change and I got caught. Mr. Tucker discovered me. He was a short, thick-shouldered, muscular masonry teacher, who the guys said had been an outstanding athlete. He was also the weightlifting coach, assigned by the principal to patrol the halls of the school during lunch periods looking for students who should be outside. "What the hell are you doing here, boy? Students aren't allowed in this area. Why aren't you outside?" Whoa! I was so taken aback I couldn't say anything. He just stared, looking me over from head to toe. He reached for my sketchpad. "Did you do these drawings?" he asked. "Yes sir," I responded. "I draw here in this area because it's quiet." He continued looking through the drawings smiling. Then he said, "Come on with me." Following behind, I knew he was taking me to the Dean's office. I just knew I was going to get expelled.

Instead, he took me to his masonry shop where he asked my name and then instructed me to sit. He wanted to know why a boy my size wasn't playing football, what I wanted to do in life, how my grades were, who my parents were and where I lived. Then he talked to me about the values of living clean and building my body through weight training. I began enjoying the way he was relating to me and I was impressed with his genuine interest. He asked if I would allow him to put me on a bodybuilding program which he would supervise. I agreed, and after school he drove me home where he met my parents. He asked them to buy a set of weights. In a few days when they responded, he followed through and became my personal coach in bodybuilding.

I followed the program he laid out religiously. Over the summer, I became obsessed with being fit and strong. I drove myself to physical limits, and then drove myself some more. I grew bigger, heavier, muscular, faster. When football season came around, I was in control of myself and more self-assured when going up against somebody. I started to like the feel of hitting. I found a groove of meanness and stayed in it. And I found that I loved to win.

ANSEL ADAMS

Photographer, Conservationist

1902–1984

 WHY ANSEL

Because he was the master photographer of the West. Ansel Adams's legendary black-and-white photos of Yosemite National Park and other natural landscapes offer visions of beauty so grand, they have become the standard by which all other nature photos are judged.

Because as a board member of the Sierra Club for nearly forty years, Adams focused on working with the government to preserve national parks.

Because America claimed Ansel Adams as its own national treasure by awarding him the prestigious National Medal of Freedom, the nation's highest civil honor.

Ansel Adams was just four years old in 1906 when San Francisco's great earthquake hit, leaving him with a broken nose and vivid memories of the power of nature. Shards of glass, collapsed chimneys, and panicked adults painted this picture of hysteria. He learned early on that the ground we stand on is not always solid.

ANSEL'S STORY:

Though usually at home with us, April 17, 1906, found my father away on business in Washington, D.C. Mr. O'Connor, an old family friend, occupied the guest room. Our Chinese cook, Kong, slept in the basement. That evening all was quiet, except for the boom of the surf pounding on Baker Beach. I was tucked away in my child's bed. Nelly, my nanny, an elderly woman of expansive heart and frame, slept next to me in her bed.

At five-fifteen the next morning, we were awakened by a tremendous noise. Our beds were moving violently about. Nelly held frantically on to mine, as together we crashed back and forth against the walls. Our west window gave way in a shower of glass, and the handsome brick chimney passed by the north window, slicing through the greenhouse my father had just completed. The roaring, swaying, moving, and grinding continued for what seemed like a long time; it actually took less than a minute. Then, there was an eerie silence with only the surf sounds coming through the shattered window and an occasional crash of plaster and tinkle of glass from downstairs.

Nelly pulled me out of bed and quickly dressed me. My mother hastened into my room; I recall her as rather pale and dazed; the entire fireplace in her room had gone with the fallen chimney and she had awakened to a broad view of the Golden Gate and the cold morning breeze. She hugged me tightly and then we hesitantly went downstairs to assess the damage.

The impressions of confusion during the following days and, above all, the differences in daily life, are still very much with me.

I recall a great to-do about cleaning up the house and a large and growing mound of broken glassware, crockery, bricks, and assorted rubble, piled in a far corner of the garden. Mr. O'Connor walked into town and secured food. Soldiers from the Presidio came by and gave us fresh water.

Kong returned to Chinatown to be with his family and friends. He came back a day later, looking grim, and stated that he had found no one and that fire was everywhere. He never discovered what happened to his family. It is probable that they were lost with the many others in the fiery holocaust that consumed most of San Francisco east of Van Ness Avenue following the earthquake. Since the principal waterways and cisterns of the city were destroyed in the quake, there was no water with which to contest the fast-spreading flames. I have heard an estimate of four hundred lives lost; it was also said that the real total was closer to four thousand, as it is probable that the Chinese had never been counted.

I can understand now the intense anxiety my father must have felt, thousands of miles away, buffeted by outrageous telegraphed rumors of total disaster. It had been variously reported that all the city had burned, that San Francisco was slowly sinking into the sea, or that a huge tidal wave had wrecked the entire Bay area. My father left Washington as soon as he could find space on a train and arrived about six days later. Finally reaching the ferry docks, he was unable to get a horse and buggy, so he ran and walked five miles around the periphery of the fire to our home. Happily, he found all was well, with his family healthy and the house he had built largely intact.

My closest experience with profound human suffering was that earthquake and fire.

CHAPTER 4

CHALLENGED TO THE MAX

Overcoming Tough Stuff

Failure is the opportunity to begin again, more intelligently.

—HENRY FORD

Gut check time. You're scared. You're pumped. Your gut says go for it. Your brain says wait. Challenges surround you daily. Count on it. They might come in the form of discussions with your parents. "How do I word this so Mom won't freak out?" Or come from that annoying kid on the bus who makes it his mission in life to torment you every morning. "I'd punch him, but then I'd be the one who gets in trouble."

Dealing with daily challenges means making choices. Making the right choice is often the most difficult challenge of all. As you know, sometimes you score big time and sometimes you'd give anything to turn back the clock, remove foot from mouth, and start over.

Bummer. But that's how you learn and grow into the confident, intelligent, and interesting man you are destined to become.

In this chapter of *The Boldness of Boys,* you will read how some of these famous men met challenges and hurdled the obstacles blocking their paths. Both Paul Orfalea, founder of Kinko's, and champion diver Greg Louganis suffered from dyslexia. Try getting through school unable to read. Tough guys who only saw a scrawny nerd in oversized clothes tormented skateboard champ Tony Hawk in school. Secretary of State Colin Powell, labeled a boy without much direction, challenged himself to excel at something, but what? Grown men slung mean jabs at ten-year-old Wayne Gretzky as he began to make hockey history in Canada. And photographer Neil Leifer took his best photo because he overcame a challenge at a famous Giants game.

Hopefully, you will relate to at least one of the stories these men share. And remember, when faced with your own challenges, ask for help when you need it. Ignore the stares. Stay focused when confronted with obstacles that seem insurmountable.

In the Chinese written language, two characters define the word "crisis." One means *danger*. The second means *opportunity*. The two go together. Your own crisis or challenge might look like danger at first. But within every crisis, there is an opportunity to seize.

TUPAC SHAKUR

Musician, Poet

1971–1996

? WHY TUPAC

Because 2Pac still rules. Even after his death from a gunshot wound at age twenty-five, the stories of heartbreak, ambition, and passion told in the music of this controversial and introspective street poet still appeal to all races.

It is said that Tupac Shakur lived his life on his terms, did not care what others thought—just simply told it like it was. Born to parents who were both members of the Black Panthers—a radical political African American group of the '60s—Tupac studied at the Baltimore School of Arts during his teen years. The family's move to California introduced Tupac to gang life. As unforgiving as it was, through every challenge, he held on to hope.

AND 2MORROW

Today is filled with anger
Fueled with hidden hate
Scared of being outcast
Afraid of common fate

CHALLENGED TO THE MAX

Today is built on tragedies
which no one wants 2 face
Nightmares 2 humanities
and morally disgraced
Tonight is filled with rage
Violence in the air
Children bred with ruthlessness
Because no one at home cares
Tonight I lay my head down
But the pressure never stops
gnawing at my sanity
content when I am dropped
But 2morrow I c change
A chance 2 build anew
Built on spirit, intent of heart
And ideals based on truth
And 2morrow I wake with second wind
And strong because of pride
2 know I fought with all my heart
2 keep my dream alive

NEIL LEIFER

Photojournalist

born: 1942

WHY NEIL

Because so many famous sports photos have been taken by Neil Leifer.

Because since 1960, over 200 of his images have graced the covers of *Sports Illustrated, Time,* and *People* magazines, making him the most published photojournalist in Time, Inc., history.

Because for fifteen Olympic Games, every gold-medal winner has been the focus of Leifer's lens.

Neil Leifer thrives on a challenge. His dad said photography was a rich man's sport that Neil wouldn't be able to afford. That's just what Neil needed to hear. To support his hobby, he immediately got a job as the delivery boy at the famous Stage Deli in New York City. Neil delivered sandwiches to the *Life* magazine office and would hang out with the famous photographers and watch them shoot. Endeared by his enthusiasm to learn, they would tip Neil with film instead of money. Seeing how the pros did it made Neil believe he could, too. When the opportunity to shoot a football game in Yankee Stadium presented itself, he seized it. A challenge? You bet. Neil ended up taking one of football's most memorable photos ever. And it happened on his sixteenth birthday.

NEIL'S STORY:

It didn't take long for me to get visions of grandeur, dreams of shooting the Rangers and the Knicks at Madison Square Garden, or the Giants or the Yankees, instead of the high school football games I'd been shooting. The problem was, to do that, I needed a press credential. No way was that going to happen. The New York press was a tight little club. No outsiders were allowed on the sidelines of a Giants game. Even if I could have afforded a ticket, which I couldn't, I would have been too far away from the action to photograph anything worthwhile.

Early in the 1958 football season, I found out that every Sunday, this veterans hospital in The Bronx brought three or four busloads of vets in wheelchairs to the game. They needed volunteers to wheel in the fifty or sixty wheelchairs and never had enough, so I volunteered. I'd be there when the buses pulled up and wheel the veterans right along the outfield end zone. They were literally on the field. Of course, I always had my camera tucked under my coat. After a few weeks of doing this, the stadium staff got to know me. As it turned cold, we'd hand out coffee to the vets and I'd bring a hot cup to the security guys guarding the bench area. Before long, they'd look the other way while I snapped a few pictures.

On December 28, 1958, the Giants ended up playing the championship game against the Baltimore Colts. I remember the date because it was my sixteenth birthday. And I'll never forget it because of the photograph I took. That game has been described as the greatest football game ever played because it put the NFL and football on the road to surpassing baseball as the most popular sport in this country. The great Johnny Unitas leading the Baltimore Colts handed the ball to Alan "the Horse" Ameche, who scored a touchdown in sudden death. By the time he scored, so many drunken Baltimore Colts fans were converging on the field, the security guards had their hands full keeping them off. I positioned myself right on the end-zone line, exactly ten yards from where Alan Ameche had scored that touchdown.

If I had any money for a decent camera, I surely would have had a long lens or a 135-millimeter, something to fill the frame, but I didn't. I had a Yashica Mat, which I call the poor man's Rolleiflex. It was a two-and-a-quarter square camera with a regular lens. Standing where I was, Alan Ameche was exactly thirty feet from me. Even at that relatively short distance, the image was very small. Within the frame, you could see almost all of the twenty-two players. You could see the shocked look on the faces of the New York Giant players. You could see the joy that was about to explode from the Baltimore Colts, including Johnny Unitas. What really made that photo was the lighting. It was a cold winter afternoon. The lights were on in the stadium and the sky was almost dark but not quite. The lighting projected a mood that made that photo special. You could see the entire façade of the old Yankee Stadium, which was such a pretty structure. It's a beautiful photo because of the mood. It was published a year later as an inside cover of a magazine, one of these annual football preview magazines. It was a great thrill seeing my name on a photo that filled an entire page of a magazine.

It's a photo that to this day is one of the best I have ever taken and I took it on my sixteenth birthday.

THE BOLDNESS OF BOYS

JACKIE CHAN

Actor, Martial Arts Master

born: 1954

❓WHY JACKIE

Because this kung fu master who has made over one hundred action films brings his fans big-time thrills with each death-defying move he makes on screen. Whether he's jumping off buildings, hanging from helicopters, or crashing through plate glass windows, Jackie Chan makes audiences gasp at his ability and howl at his jokes.

Because Asia's biggest box office draw and America's adopted son performs his own adrenaline-pumping stunts in action films like *Rush Hour*, *Shanghai Noon*, *Shanghai Knights*, and *The Tuxedo*.

Because courage and comedy wrapped in youthful exuberance make Chan a superstar who has already received a Lifetime Achievement Award from MTV and earned a star on Hollywood's Walk of Fame.

Jackie Chan's father was a cook and his mother kept house for the French Embassy in Hong Kong where Chan was born. His father relocated to Australia but before leaving, he enrolled his seven-year-old son in the China Drama Academy. For the next ten years, the academy educated and groomed Chan to be a dancer, singer, gymnast, and martial arts expert. At first, Chan loved the notion of being able to practice martial arts all day long, but for the ten years that he was there, Jackie Chan was brutally punished and criticized when his moves didn't meet his master's expectations.

JACKIE'S STORY:

The system we lived under at the school was simple and straightforward. Master believed in just three things: discipline, hard work, and order. Discipline came quickly and painfully, measured in strokes of a cane. Hard work was the rule of the day—a few minutes of stolen rest often meant an hour of practice for the unlucky students caught slacking off. And order: order was imposed by a strict line of command that placed Master at the top (never to be disobeyed or disrespected); then his wife, Madame; followed by the instructors who taught singing, boxing, and weapons skills; and then the students at the bottom.

Even among the students there was an order. Each of us was ranked by seniority, with the Biggest Brother (the one who had been at the school the longest) at the top, and the Littlest (the newest student) at the very bottom of the entire heap.

The order was never to be challenged. If a brother who was more senior told you to do something, you did it. If you told a more junior brother to do something, he did it. And if Master gave a command, *everybody* jumped. The order was enforced by the fact that anyone who disobeyed it was beaten soundly, either by the master's cane or, among students, by the simpler (but not any less painful!) means of a hard-swung fist. . . .

Training would go on until bedtime, which was midnight. All of us students from the six-year-old newcomers to the Biggest Brothers and Sisters, had the same schedule: 5 A.M. to 12 A.M., five hours of sleep and then another day of training—day after day, seven days a week. Free time was rare and a cause for celebration; opportunities to go out, away from the academy, were even rarer. So, until we grew old and skilled enough to perform, the gray walls of the China Drama Academy were nearly all the world we knew. . . .

But I had nowhere to run. My mother couldn't have taken care of me on her own, and anyway, if I'd gone back to the mansion on the Peak, I wouldn't have had anything to do. I was too young to work, and I wasn't suited for school. The academy was the only place where my abilities could be developed into something worthwhile, the only place where I had a future.

ARTHUR ASHE
Professional Tennis Player, Activist, Author

1943–1993

? WHY ARTHUR

Because Arthur Ashe, one of America's most distinguished tennis players, brought character and class to the courts.

Because he was the first African American to join the U.S. Davis Cup team and win a U.S tennis championship. Because while he was ranked the number one tennis player in the world, he spoke out for players' rights, forming the Association of Tennis Professionals.

Because Ashe faced major health issues after retiring from tennis. In spite of two open-heart surgeries—one that infected him with HIV—he continued to speak out on race relations, apartheid, and AIDS until his death at age fifty.

Because he was black in a predominantly white sport, Arthur Ashe had an image to uphold. Be polite. Don't cause trouble. As he got older, maintaining his reputation became his biggest concern. During the '60s, as he was coming up through the ranks, his semiliterate father tried hard to protect his son from the hate so prevalent in that time. The subtle pressures of racism proved to be a challenge throughout Ashe's life.

ARTHUR'S STORY:

I am best when I keep my ego under tight control and try to reason and look ahead, beyond temporary, flashy victories at some other human being's expense, to the future. One consequence of my commitment to reasoning and reconciling would always be to have some people think of me as conservative, or opportunistic, or even a coward. So be it.

Needless to say, there were times when I asked myself whether I was being principled or simply a coward. While I was growing up, I was undoubtedly timid away from the tennis court. I was not only my father's child; I was wrapped in the cocoon of tennis early in life, mainly by blacks like my most powerful mentor, Dr. Robert Walter Johnson of Lynchburg, Virginia. They insisted that I be unfailingly polite on the court, unfalteringly calm and detached, so that whites could never accuse me of meanness. I learned well. I look at photographs of the skinny, frail, little black boy that I was in the early 1950s, and I see that I was my tennis racquet and my tennis racquet was me. It was my rod and my staff.

Looking out for his two motherless sons, my father tried to keep us out of harm's way, and the possibility of harm was real. We all knew what had happened to Emmett Till, whose death in 1955 cast a shadow over my youth and that of virtually all black kids in Richmond and no doubt across America. Fourteen years old and from Chicago, Emmett was visiting his family in Mississippi when, on a dare according to reports, he whistled at a white woman. White men came for him at his uncle's house, took him away, murdered him, mutilated his body, and dumped it in a river. We assumed that the Ku Klux Klan was to blame. Virginia was not Mississippi, but the Klan was with us, too. It could happen to any of us.

My father respected the skilled, courageous leaders in the black community of Richmond, including lawyers such as Oliver Hill and Spottswood Robinson III, who had strong connections to the legal side of the movement; but protesting was for other people. He himself worked hard at his humble jobs, and tried to get along with everyone. He followed the unfolding saga of civil rights as best he could and he recognized that freedom for blacks was at stake and that we had to fight for it, but he made sure that my brother and I never risked our lives against anyone, much less the police or the Klan.

PAUL ORFALEA
Founder of Kinko's Copy Center

born: 1947

? WHY PAUL

Because the idea Paul Orfalea thought of in college exploded into the largest photocopy center in the world—over eleven hundred Kinko's stores. Orfalea opened his first shop in a shack so tiny, they had to drag the machine out to the sidewalk to do business. The name Kinko's came from his curly red hair.

Because Paul Orfalea has dyslexia. He struggled throughout his school years, and reading is still extremely difficult for him.

Because the Orfalea Family Foundation generously conributes to educational institutions.

Paul Orfalea knows about challenges. Getting C's and D's in school was as good as it was going to get. Even though he suffered from dyslexia, which severely hampered his ability to read, he did not allow it to get in the way of his ambition. At that time, not much was known about teaching dyslexic kids, but Paul managed to get through high school and college by tapping into his listening skills and by taking classes that didn't require much reading.

PAUL'S STORY:

Not many kids flunk the second grade, but I did. It wasn't that my school was especially hard, or that I was lazy, or that my teacher was cruel and inhuman, although I certainly thought so at the time. I just couldn't read. I was dyslexic, but nobody knew that back then. It wasn't that dyslexia hadn't been invented—it just wasn't recognized as a medical condition. People just thought you were dumb or lazy.

In second grade, we were taught to read. My fellow students had no trouble breaking the code I found so mysterious. When called upon to read aloud in class, they read as though angels whispered words in their ears. When they wrote, their fingers made graceful curves and straight lines teachers could understand and praise. Mine made chicken tracks. Were my fellow students from a different planet? Did they have a special gift? Or were they faking it and really having as much trouble as I?

I was confused and embarrassed. At seven, I was a curly-headed Lebanese kid who knew too much about anxiety and shame. To a dyslexic, a sentence is not like Egyptian hieroglyphics or a cryptogram. It's more like a road map with mouse holes or coffee stains in critical places. With a map like that, you're always turning into blind alleys and ending up on the wrong side of town.

For third grade, I was sent to a school for what was then called retarded children. My classmates had Down's syndrome and other severe conditions of mental impairment. The small class was held in a woman's backyard in Hollywood. I remember her to be mean, but maybe she was just strict. My stay there didn't last long. My mother had me tested, and when my IQ was fixed at 130, it was decided that maybe I wasn't with my peer group after all. But that didn't mean I didn't need serious help.

My next few years were filled with desperate efforts on my parents' part to help their afflicted son. I was assigned to special reading groups, sent to speech therapists, examined by psychologists and eye doctors.

It didn't help that in addition to my dyslexia, I had "behavior problems." I loved mischief and got in trouble at every opportunity. I might not be able to decipher a complicated written document, but I could have found my way to the principal's office blindfolded.

Meanwhile, my grades were terrible. I was getting D's and F's in school, yet my parents never made an issue of grades. They never made me feel stupid.

I attended practically every high school in Los Angeles at one time or another and was usually asked to leave by an outraged principal. It was like a hotel, check-in, check-out. I was not a juvenile delinquent or a danger to others, but I was disruptive, difficult, and easily bored. And most damning was the fact that at the ages of eighteen and nineteen, I still couldn't read.

Called the formative years of childhood, as I look back on them, I can see that I was definitely being formed. Those who knew me might have thought I was being malformed by humiliation, frustration, and fear. In spite of having a supportive family, I was often alone and guessed that the future didn't look bright for somebody like me.

ERNIE BARNES

Artist, Former Professional Football Player

born: 1938

 **WHY ERNIE**

Because Ernie Barnes played center, tackle, and guard for the Baltimore Colts, the San Diego Chargers, and the Denver Broncos.

Because he has always looked at life as an artist, even when he was playing professional football. Known today as one of America's most respected contemporary figurative painters, Ernie Barnes has combined his two passions by depicting athletic events in his art.

Because Barnes chose to become a full-time artist in 1965, when the owner of the New York Jets commissioned him to do a series of paintings for more money than he had ever earned in football.

Ernie Barnes was a tormented child. Almost daily, school thugs bullied him. Creating art was the reward he gave himself for surviving through another day. Armed with a vivid imagination, his pencil in hand, Barnes drew a life that was tolerable, even magical at times . . . that is, until the next day at school.

ERNIE'S STORY:

Children born under the sign of Cancer, as I was, reportedly receive their best grades in art, can be overly dramatic, treasure the past, are mother's little darlings and get only fair grades in mathematics. They are also sensitive. It was with these credentials that I entered the first grade. By law, I was thrown in with a pocket of kids who were overlooked when such virtues as gentility and good manners were passed out. They hated me. My mother escorted me to school ten times before I could accept the fact that I had to stay there. I couldn't conform easily to the athletic ideal and was made to feel inadequate. I wasn't able to fight, to run fast, nor was I picked for rough games. I was introverted and shy.

After school, fights were daily. Wherever I turned, I was beset with a thorny dilemma. My well-groomed appearance, my fat body and mild attitude made me a target for anyone needing a notch on their belt. Bullies would circle me and push me from one side to the other, once causing my trombone case to fly open and I had to run around chasing the boy trying to blow it through the wrong end. I must have looked so stupid pleading for them to stop pushing me. I was completely scared. Spinning around amid a kaleidoscope of blurred faces, I was trying hard to keep from crying. Already I had scraped my knee when I slid into the gravel. My hands were bleeding and for the first time, down deep inside, I was angry with my mother for dressing me in the same fashion as the White kids who went to the fashionable private schools. My knee-length socks, short pants, and sweater with a cap to match didn't impress Leroy, John and Nathaniel, who all had to wear military clothes. Mama also took great satisfaction in having me parade my wardrobe in front of her friends. "Good evening, ladies. I'm Ernest, Jr.," I was required to say while taking a bow. "Oh, he's so cute. Fannie, you have such darling children." The last thing I wanted to do was to be a "darling" because it was getting me killed.

It reached the point where I was no longer concerned with the pain I was suffering. My heartfelt concern was when it would end. If there was a day that I did not come home in tears because of a fight, it could be attributed to sickness, the weekend, or it was rained out. I was beaten so severely, my mother requested that I be allowed to leave school fifteen minutes before the other kids. Permission was granted. When I was at home and drawing, I was happy. My senses addressed themselves naturally to the discovery of what I could make happen on paper. It was so easy. From the shrouded mists of my sensitivity, I made friends with lines, allowing them to flow into things belonging to my immediate environment: the trees, clouds, birds and people. In school, nobody laughed and made fun of me when I was drawing. They just watched in silent awe.

JOHN McCAIN
United States Senator
born: 1936

? WHY JOHN

Because as the U.S. senator from Arizona and a one-time presidential candidate, John McCain devotes his life to public service.

Because he learned firsthand about human suffering during the Vietnam War when his plane was shot down and he was held as a prisoner-of-war in Hanoi for five and a half years, much of that time in solitary confinement.

Because Captain John McCain served in the navy for twenty-two years before retiring in 1981.

John McCain grew up a navy brat, which meant his family moved often during his childhood. Though he

welcomed the change, making new friends was a constant challenge. Who would be a friend? Who would be
a foe? Saying good-bye to the friends he had made
never got any easier. That's why Senator McCain appre-
ciates the value of a true friend.

JOHN'S STORY:

Like my father and grandfather, I lacked as a boy the
physical size to appear imposing on first acquaintance.
Together with the challenges of my transient childhood,
my small stature motivated me to prove quickly to new
schoolmates that I could stand up for myself. The
quickest way to do so was to fight the first kid who pro-
voked me.

Whether I won or lost those fights wasn't as important as establishing myself as someone who could
adapt to the challenges of a new environment without
betraying apprehension. I foolishly believed that fighting,
as well as challenging school authorities and ignoring
school regulations, was indispensable to my self-esteem
and helped me to form new friendships.

The repeated farewells to friends rank among the
saddest regrets of a childhood constantly disrupted by

the demands of my father's career. I would arrive at a new school, go to considerable lengths to make new friends, and, shortly thereafter, be transplanted to a new town to begin the process all over again. Seldom if ever did I see again the friends I left behind. If you have never known any other life, these experiences seem a natural part of existence. You come to expect friendships to last but a short time. I believe this breeds in a child a desire to make the most of friendships while they last. The relationships make up with intensity what they lack in length. That's one of the benefits of an itinerant childhood.

WAYNE GRETZKY
Former Professional Hockey Player
born: 1961

? WHY WAYNE

Because Wayne Gretzky dominated the National Hockey League (NHL) for twenty seasons.

Because he helped Canada's Edmonton Oilers win four Stanley Cup Championships.

Because Gretzky rules as leader in goals and assists, and when he was traded to the Los Angeles Kings, he made hockey a major sports attraction in California for seven seasons.

Because of his greatness, when Gretzky retired in 1999 from the New York Rangers, his jersey number (99) was retired, too, a first in the NHL.

Nothing could have stopped Wayne Gretzky from breaking every hockey record when he was a kid. But why did people have to be so mean? His challenges were different from those of your average ten-year-old. From his first glide on the ice, Wayne was a star. That fact exposed an ugly side of parents watching from the sidelines. They jeered and insulted him. He had to rise above it, a lot to handle for a little kid.

WAYNE'S STORY:

And then came the year that was a dream and a nightmare at the same time. It was the first time unhappiness really crept into my life. I was ten years old, still four feet four, and I scored 378 goals in sixty-nine games. I won the scoring race by 238 goals.

. . . But those 378 goals were the beginning of the end for me in Brantford. First of all, it created national attention. By the age of ten, I'd done more interviews than some NHL players. . . .

Anyway, that 378 started people's minds to warping.

There was even a wild rumor that the New York Rangers were going to buy the entire Brantford Pee Wee franchise, just so they'd have first rights to me when I turned pro. *Right.* All that publicity and attention on a ten-year-old was getting hard to handle. Hockey was no longer just fun. It became fun mixed with doses of fame and jealousy and ugliness. . . .

My sudden stardom didn't set too well with the parents of the other kids. . . . To an extent, now I can understand where those parents were coming from. Maybe I was a little showy. I was ten years old and I had my now-famous "kick" when I'd score a goal. I'd kick my knee up high and bring my right arm down like I was pulling down on a train whistle. But I wasn't trying to be cocky. I got it from a guy in my dad's Junior B league where he coached. His name was Dave Pay and he played for St. Catherine's. I don't think he ever even made it to pro hockey, but I was a stick boy in that league and I thought everything Dave Pay did was cool, so I started doing it.

I guess parents were just trying to protect their own kids' development in hockey. . . . I've thought about it now as an adult, and I think if I really had been a selfish player, my teammates wouldn't have liked me. But that just wasn't true. It was always the parents. One day the goalie had only five shots on goal the whole game and he let in three. We lost 3–2. His father came up to me afterward and called me every name in the book. Parents would sit in the stands and do nothing but scream at me. I never understood why a parent would do that. I mean, did they ever stop and think how that made *their* kid feel?

They were all sure I was going to be exposed as talentless. All along the way, people just couldn't accept what I was doing. They'd see the numbers, the 378s, and just refuse to believe they were real. "It's got to be a fluke," they'd say, and they kept saying it. When I was ten, they were saying I'd be washed up at twelve. When I was twelve, they were saying I'd be washed up by fourteen. When I was fourteen, they said fifteen. It became a good luck charm in our family. As long as people were saying I was doomed, we knew we were in good shape.

DANNY VILLANUEVA

Former Professional Football Player, Business Executive, Philanthropist

born: 1937

❓ WHY DANNY

Because he was the placekicker for the Los Angeles Rams from 1960 to 1964 and for the Dallas Cowboys from 1965 to 1967, and still holds several NFL kicking records.

Because during his playing years, Danny Villanueva worked part-time as a news director at KMEX-TV in Los Angeles. Moving up the corporate ladder, he became general manager and then president, turning KMEX into the most profitable Spanish-speaking television station in the United States.

Because his involvement with the Spanish-language television networks Univision and Telemundo changed the face of Spanish television.

Because Villanueva is passionate about young people and works with several nonprofits aimed at helping them stay in school.

Danny Villanueva and his brothers had their mother to contend with if they misbehaved or lost a football game. They could handle that. Listening to slurs about their religious beliefs wasn't as easy to take. His challenge was to learn tolerance—not to judge people by their character, or their skin color, or their heritage, or their religion.

DANNY'S STORY:

I was the first one in the family to graduate from college. We grew up right in the center of Calexico. My mother used sports as a way to discipline us. My brothers and I all played. She used it to keep us in line, to keep us out of trouble. We went from one sport to another year-round. She encouraged that. She made her presence felt. She very seldom went to a game. But she would listen to the radio. She didn't know what the guy was saying, but she knew numbers because she used to go to Safeway. In the end, they would say, "El Centro, 30, Calexico, 10," and she knew that. And then we would get punished. She'd make us sit outside for a while. And if we won, the lights would be on, the doors would be open, and we'd have dinner. But if we lost, we had to think a little bit about it.

Our lives revolved around sports and the church. It was not easy because we were Protestants— Methodists—and that made it difficult because most everyone in town was Catholic. There was a lot of intolerance. Some of the roughest times were over religious differences. We were a minority within a minority. It was not easy. You want to be accepted and you're not. Kids would chase us home sometimes, and then they'd say things during our church services or throw rocks at us. It had a lasting impact on me. That's something I've carried with me all my life. I know firsthand that tolerance is a wonderful virtue.

KELLY SLATER

World Champion Surfer

born: 1972

? WHY KELLY

Because he's number one, the man to beat. No one compares to this winner of six surfing world titles.

Because he took time off in 1990 to get even smarter and now he's back on the board, riding waves, winning competitions, with his new thirty-year-old perspective.

Today, Kelly Slater actually roots for his competition. Not so in the old days. Back then, he tried to demoralize his opponents. His newfound attitude could be a by-product of age, or maybe of winning so many world titles, but Kelly Slater is now more willing to share. After years of analyzing his every move in surfing, he handles his current challenges by staying in the moment—one wave at a time.

KELLY'S STORY:

Lately, a lot of things just seem to have fallen into place for me and I think it's because I've just surrendered and now keep my focus on each moment while I'm riding a wave.

If I want to win the world title, I have to ask myself how I am going to do that. I have to break the competition down into its components. I start out by realizing I have to win all three heats to do well in the event. I have to study the guy I'm competing against. I think about how I can improve my performance. I think about the right equipment I'll need. Then I just break it down further and further. At points, I would get to a place where I wasn't thinking about anything ahead at all. I was only thinking about the next stroke I was going to take, paddling.

I remember this happened in '95, I was really trailing. I had won two world titles, and it was really important to me to win a third because three has always been my lucky number. I won in '92, then I didn't win in '93, and it really kind of hurt me. I wondered if the first one was a fluke. Could I back it up? It's really rare for someone to win a world title and then win another world title the next year. So, I wanted to do that. I won the second one in '94, and it was really important to me in '95 to win back-to-back titles, to really prove my point.

I had a heat in a contest where a guy had gotten a perfect score on his first wave. It's really hard to beat somebody who has a perfect score on a wave because you have to get two extremely high scores to beat them. Everything just turned my way because of my "think about each moment" approach. On the next ride, I almost got a perfect score. Then, I got another one, and he ended up getting another score of only two points. So he had a ten and a two, and I had two nine-point rides. I thought, "Wow, I'm going to trust this thing." Then, I won the event, and I started kind of coming back.

At the end of '95, I did the same thing. It was my last event of the year and I had to get second in the event in order to win the world title. There were two people ahead of me. Depending on how they did, they could outright beat me. The guy who was ahead lost his first heat, totally out of the blue. Everything went wrong for him. The guy he was competing against was even trying to help him win the heat because he wanted him to win the world title. It totally backfired on him. Then, I went head-to-head against the other guy, and I ended up having to win the contest in order to win the title. I did, and it was the last event of the year. Everything just came together perfectly. I surrendered to the situation, kept my focus—and I think that really helped.

COLIN POWELL

**Secretary of State,
G. W. Bush Administration**

born: 1937

 WHY COLIN

Because he represents what an American can accomplish in this great land of opportunity. After a stellar career in the army, the son of Jamaican immigrants served as the twelfth chairman of the Joint Chiefs of Staff in 1989 to 1993, the highest military position in the Department of Defense. During his chairmanship, Powell oversaw operations in the Persian Gulf War.

Because in 2001, this decorated hero became secretary of state under the George W. Bush administration. Secretary Colin Powell is a symbol of honor.

During elementary and high school, Colin Powell's challenges were those of most kids: trying to do well in school and hang with the cool kids, while working part-time jobs here and there. Though he had the love and support of his family, his first real opportunity to challenge himself arrived in the form of a uniform when he entered City College of New York (CCNY) and joined the Reserve Officers' Training Corps (ROTC).

COLIN'S STORY:

When I was nine, catastrophe struck the Powell family. As a student at P.S. 39, I passed from the third to the fourth grade but into the bottom form, "Four Up," a euphemism meaning the kid is a little slow. This was the sort of secret to be whispered with shaking heads in our family circle. Education was the escape hatch, the way up and out for West Indians. My sister was already an excellent student, destined for college. And here I was, having difficulty in the fourth grade. I lacked drive, not ability. I was a happy-go-lucky kid, amenable, amiable, and aimless. . . .

I did, however, stand out in one arena. I was an excellent acolyte and subdeacon, and enjoyed my ecclesiastical duties. Here was organization, tradition, hierarchy, pageantry, purpose—a world, now that I think about it, not much unlike the Army. . . .

During my first semester at CCNY, something had caught my eye—young guys on campus in uniform. CCNY was a hotbed of liberalism, radicalism, even some leftover communism from the thirties; it was not a place where you would expect much of a military presence. When I returned to school in the fall of 1954, I inquired about the Reserve Officers' Training Corps, and I enlisted in ROTC. . . .

There came a day when I stood in line in the drill hall to be issued olive-drab pants and jacket, brown shirt, brown tie, brown shoes, a belt with a brass buckle, and an overseas cap. As soon as I got home, I put the uniform on and looked in the mirror. I liked what I saw. At this point not a single Kelly Street kid was going to college. I was seventeen. I felt cut off and lonely. The uniform gave me a sense of belonging, and something I had never experienced all the while I was growing up; I felt distinctive.

GREG LOUGANIS
Olympic and World Champion Diver
born: 1960

❓ WHY GREG

Because he's considered the world's greatest diver. Greg Louganis was the first person in fifty-six years to win Olympic gold medals in both springboard and platform events. He was also the first to win the gold in two consecutive Olympics.

Because he's a six-time world champion and has held forty-seven national championships.

Because he came home from the 1988 Olympics with the Maxwell House/U.S. Olympic Committee Spirit Award, given to athletes who demonstrate courage and contribute significantly to their sport.

Because Louganis has HIV and became a valiant spokesperson for gay rights and AIDS victims after the release of his autobiography, *Breaking the Surface*.

The silver lining to Greg Louganis's troubled youth was his emerging talent as a diver. He was only ten when he first started to dive competitively and just sixteen when he won his first Olympic medal. The downtime between competitions was tough on Louganis. Adopted into his family, he was not fully informed about his heritage and was picked on at school because of his skin color. He stuttered and had trouble reading. This challenging combination of circumstances left Louganis feeling angry and alone.

GREG'S STORY:

School was hardly a refuge from what was going on at home. As soon as Despina started school, I couldn't wait to go. She brought home books, and she had new friends. I thought it would be a lot of fun, like my acrobatics classes. Well it wasn't. From almost the first day at Chase Elementary School the other kids started calling me names. At first they teased me because I stuttered, and they called me "nigger" because my Samoan complexion got very dark in the San Diego sun. Almost all the kids at my school were white. . . .

Because of my stutter, I was put in a speech-therapy class. Most of the kids in that class were mentally impaired in addition to having speech impediments. I didn't feel like I belonged there, but I had this problem, so I thought that I must be like them, that I must be retarded too. After I got put into a special reading class, the other kids started calling me "retard." From the start, I had trouble reading, but it got really bad once we got past single words and simple sentences. Unfortunately, the special class didn't help. I got frustrated and withdrew into my shell and wouldn't talk. After school, I went to my room and closed my door.

My teachers sent me home with books for Mom to read with me, and she tried to help me. But that was even more frustrating, because she tried to show me how to read the way she read, the way most people read. What I couldn't explain—and what I didn't real-ize—was that I was dyslexic. I couldn't explain that I read a sentence forward, then backward, then forward again before I could get the letters and the words in order, so I could figure out what the sentence meant. It never occurred to me to say anything about the way I read, because I just thought I was a little slower than other people. I thought this until my dyslexia was diagnosed in college.

TONY HAWK
Professional Skateboarder

born: 1968

❓ WHY TONY

Because the man virtually flies upside down while a skateboard stays glued to his feet.

Because Tony Hawk became a household name and introduced the world to professional skateboarding. Hawk went pro at the age of fourteen and by sixteen was the best skateboarder in the world. He's the master of such daunting moves as the ollie 540, the kick-flip 540, the varial 720, and the 900.

Because in 1999, Hawk landed the first-ever 900 (two and a half midair spins) at the Summer X Games.

As a teenager Tony Hawk was all attitude. Picked on at school, his "geeky" skateboard attire was like a red flag waving for the resident jocks. They were relentless. So was Tony. His desire to win got him smacked around in gym class, but he couldn't help himself. He loved a challenge.

TONY'S STORY:

While I was learning to adapt to the skating world, I was failing miserably in the real world. Doing your own thing during elementary school is one thing; nobody's going to really hassle you. But once you get into the big leagues of high school, it's a whole different ball game.

Forget that I skated (still not cool); because of my genetics I was doomed from the start. If you think I'm skinny now, you should have seen me in the seventh grade when I was growing! Birds could have used me for nesting material. Muscle tone was something I'd only read about. I was also so short, I could have shopped in Baby Gap. I was twelve years old, barely over four feet tall, and weighed in at a freakish eighty pounds (and that was after a big meal). I could have handled the eighty-pound deal if I'd at least looked my age, with some facial hair or a deeper voice, but I resembled an anorexic ten-year-old. I was a walking noodle.

My walking skeleton physique wouldn't have been so bad if I'd continued going to a normal school, but after Farb Middle School I had to cross the tracks and head into the bigger world of Serra High School, a notoriously rough place. I was the smallest kid in school. It was considered a high school, but it included eighth and ninth graders. I barely looked old enough to be in the eighth grade. I was a bottom-feeder.

I think I may have a chemical imbalance, because once I entered the gym class I forgot about my stature and my overactive competitive gland took over. It must be as big as a grapefruit or something. My need-for-a-victory complex would flare up, making me temporarily insane. I focused on winning like I'd been focusing on skateboarding for the past few years. Never mind that kids in my class doubled me in body weight; I still needed to win. In basketball I'd run to the hoop like a torpedo, only to be flicked aside like a pesky fly. Once, in flag football, I was running for a touchdown with the class bully, a huge kid whose neck was about the same diameter as my thigh, chasing me. I scored the touchdown, stopped in the end zone, and turned around just in time to see him moments before impact. I tried to spurt out that I had already scored the touchdown and that technically this was "flag football," which meant no tackling, but the teacher wasn't looking and I was pretty much a bug on the guy's windshield as he slammed me. I lay in the dirt as he got off me and walked away. But at least I scored.

Skateboarding saved me. As humiliating as Serra was, my life rotated around Del Mar and other skaters. If I'd been dependent on school for a social life, I'd have been seriously depressed. My obsession prevented me from making scholastic friends, and the life at the skatepark overrode any sort of school socializing. I maintained good grades and attended advanced math and English classes, but I usually just put my head down, did my schoolwork, and headed straight to the skatepark after school.

CHAPTER 5

DEEP
BENCH

Mentors Who Matter

> You must give some time to your fellow man.
> Even if it's a little thing, do something for others—
> something for which you get no pay but the priv-
> ilege of doing it.
>
> —ALBERT SCHWEITZER

Some people give the gift of themselves. Mentors are like that. They get it when you don't. They listen when you're not being heard. And it's not just lip service—their actions speak louder than words. Mentors are people who make a difference by taking time to care.

The men in this chapter talk about the "deep bench" of people who made a difference in their lives. Movie director James Cameron remembered the high school teacher who believed in his potential even when he didn't. When graphic designer Milton Glaser reluctantly confessed to his science teacher that he wanted to be an artist and not a scientist his teacher supported Glaser's decision instead of trying to change his mind. Kind gestures like these make a difference in the shaping of a human being.

Believe it or not, you can be a mentor, too. There are lots of younger kids who see you as a role model. They admire a young man who is already accomplishing what they would like to. A third grader notices how well you read aloud at the podium. He respects your commitment to study in the library after school. A budding basketball player is in awe watching you pass and shoot so effortlessly. They observe how you handle yourself and they are impressed. Take time to help these younger kids. Make friends with a boy at school who sits by himself at lunch. Remember how it feels. Think about the older students you admired when you were younger. That cool camp counselor who told gross jokes and seemed to know everything there was to know about camping outdoors could be you in the future.

Keep your mind open. Look at your own deep bench of family members, teachers, and older friends who care about the decisions you make—the people who are there when you ask for help. It's hard to do it all on your own. Find a mentor who matters and then pass it forward to someone who wants to be just like you.

MILTON GLASER
Graphic Designer

born: 1929

❓ WHY MILTON

Because the master of graphic design's "I Love [heart symbol] NY" logo has become an internationally recognized icon.

Because Milton Glaser's vision and design sense compel us to pick up certain items in stores.

Because his work has appeared in museums and private collections all over the world.

Milton Glaser's earliest childhood memories include a love of art, though he also excelled in science. When he had to decide on which high school to attend, a simple comment made by an influential teacher had a great impact on Milton Glaser's young life.

MILTON'S STORY:

In those days, there was an extraordinary commitment to teaching and you could get a wonderful education in New York. Just the idea that this privilege was available to everybody was so extraordinary. I enjoyed school very much and was, generally speaking, a good student.

Early on, I was identified as an artist but had a talent for biology as well. I had a science teacher in junior high school who wanted me to go to the Bronx Science School, which was the premiere high school in the United States. At the end of the year, I told him I wanted to become an artist and attend the High School of Music and Art, which was another extraordinary school in New York. A week or two later, he stopped me in the hall and said, "I want to see you in my office." I thought he was going to dress me down for choosing art over science but when I walked into his classroom, he reached into his desk and pulled out a box of French Conté crayons. "Do good work" is all he said. Though I was not doing what he wanted me to do, he respected me enough to offer encouragement. The impact of his words strengthened our bond and made me work even harder to justify his faith in me. It was an extremely powerful moment that proved to be very important in my life.

GREG LOUGANIS
Olympic and World Champion Diver
born: 1960

? WHY GREG

Because he's considered the world's greatest diver. Greg Louganis was the first person in fifty-six years to win Olympic gold medals in both springboard and platform events. He was also the first to win the gold in two consecutive Olympics.

Because he's a six-time world champion and has held forty-seven national championships.

Because he came home from the 1988 Olympics with the Maxwell House/U.S. Olympic Committee Spirit Award, given to athletes who demonstrate courage and contribute significantly to their sport.

Because Louganis has HIV and became a valiant spokesperson for gay rights and AIDS victims after the release of his autobiography, *Breaking the Surface*.

At three years old, Greg Louganis was already comfortable competing in dance and gymnastics. Concerned that he might break his neck in gymnastics, Louganis's mother signed him up for diving lessons. This talent finally sparked an interest from his father, but it was his first coach who made Louganis perform with confidence. His earnest encouragement felt good. At last, Louganis had found someone who believed in him no matter how well he scored.

GREG'S STORY:

John Anders, a local police officer, often came by to watch us practice. One afternoon, Dad struck up a conversation with him, and it turned out that John used to be a diver and did some coaching on the side. My father later called him up and asked him if he'd consider coaching our team. . . .

John was wonderful, encouraging in a way that made us all want to do well. He took time to explain things to us and presented diving in a way that made a lot of sense to me, like the dance instructor who taught me to visualize. John said that he once had a coach who told him that diving should be like poetry, each movement flowing into the next. He also taught us to "ride the board." He said that when you push off into your hurdle, you should hear the board bounce twice against the fulcrum before you land on it. So I started listening for the board, and pretty soon I learned to ride it. That's the first step toward doing a good dive.

John was a very soft-spoken family man. I was impressed with the way he went camping and hiking with his sons. I envied John's sons, because he was the kind of father I wanted. They spent a lot of time doing the things fathers and sons do together. My father always made me feel like I was putting him out, that I was a bother, that he'd rather be doing other things than spending time with me. . . .

Coach Anders, on the other hand, always gave us the sense that he cared, that he wanted to be there with us, and that he wanted us to do our best. At the same time, as long as we did our best, it didn't matter to John whether or not we won. He made us feel good about getting second or third place. No matter how we placed, he would concentrate on the best dive we had done in that competition and praise us for doing it so well. Of course, for me, that really made me want to win so I could please him even more. Because he made me feel good about myself, I looked forward to practice, even when it was cold and I didn't feel much like diving. If every coach and gym teacher had those values, we'd see a lot fewer problems with young athletes.

ERNIE BARNES
Artist, Former Professional Football Player
born: 1938

? WHY ERNIE

Because Ernie Barnes played center, tackle, and guard for the Baltimore Colts, the San Diego Chargers, and the Denver Broncos.

Because he has always looked at life as an artist, even when he was playing professional football. Known today as one of America's most respected contemporary figurative painters, Ernie Barnes has combined his two passions by depicting athletic events in his art.

Because Barnes chose to become a full-time artist in 1965, when the owner of the New York Jets commissioned him to do a series of paintings for more money than he had ever earned in football.

A teacher who also served as one of Ernie Barnes's mentors told him this, "One must experience life in order to become an artist."

ERNIE'S STORY:

The chairman of the art department at North Carolina College was Ed Wilson, who had been an apprentice to the noted sculptor William Zorack. Winston B. Fletcher was the co-chairman and between them, they lent a great depth of integrity to art education. They had the wisdom to combine all of their knowledge in classes, which taught the fundamentals of drawing and painting, anatomy, structure, drapery, perspective, light and shade, sculpture, basic design, study of the figure and art history. Since the entire program was designed to lead gracefully into an individual style, they were on a constant search for individuality. What a place! I practically lived in this building, often cutting classes to absorb as much knowledge as possible. I loved walking into the big studio classroom and smelling the oils and seeing the easels standing in wait. . . .

Wilson said to me, "If you're going to be an artist, you've got to work from your experiences, whatever they might be. When you're on the field, check out what's going on around you in that muggy conflict. Feel the solidity of those bumps; pay attention to what you're going through, then tell me about it. When you walk around, what do you see? What moves you? I want to know your opinion about it." Wilson had played football at the University of Iowa. Through him, I came to better understand the art process and the athletic process as being parts of one entity. I knew that I did not stop being an artist when I was on the football field. There was no separation in me. . . .

Once, when I was struggling for an idea to paint, he became upset and asked me, "Where do you live?" I was puzzled. After telling him, he had me put on my jacket and we left class. Saying little, I joined him in his car with his explanation: "We're going for a little drive to your neighborhood." I wondered why. On the way he said, "Art is about life and how you feel about it. It's not something that's separate and apart from life. You serve as being a kind of a reporter of your discoveries and opinions about life. Don't ever tell me that you don't know what to paint. That's like telling me that you have no opinion, that you don't think or feel about anything."

We got out of the car in front of the two-story, imitation-brick house which was my home and proceeded to walk down the unpaved stretch of dirt and rocks I knew as Willard Street. Suddenly he stopped and began to unearth an old shoe, buried below the surface. We both pulled at it until we jerked it free. "Now," he said, standing back and then walking to back to position the shoe. "There is a story. That shoe has been places. It has kicked, nudged, gotten wet, been run in, danced in, gotten snowed on and run over. It's endured so much it separated from its other half. Somebody just had to give up on it. Now look at your shoes." I looked down at my practically new desert boots. It was very much in style, as reflected by the number of guys who wore them on campus. Not only on my campus, but over at Duke and UNC. "Those shoes," he said while approaching me and pointing toward my feet. "Those shoes don't know shit. They haven't been any place. They haven't experienced the vulgarities of struggle of that old shoe. That's what you paint. That story and the story of these old, weather-scarred homes. Art is all around you. Use what you see. You catch my drift?"

JAY LENO

Comedian and talk show host

born: 1950

WHY JAY

Because "the king of late night" has delivered the punch line for over ten years as the host of *The Tonight Show*.

Because Jay Leno worked the nightclub circuit 300 nights a year before making it big on TV. He still tours to college campuses and venues around the United States and plays for troops overseas.

Growing up in Andover, Massachusetts, is where Jay Leno got his first notion that he might be able to break into the entertainment industry. He was always cracking jokes at school and trying out new material on teachers and students. Voted class clown consistently, he was encouraged by one teacher to stick with it.

JAY'S STORY:

For some unimaginable reason, a handful of my teachers didn't give up on me as a hopeless moron. Mr. Robicheaud, my history teacher, never doubted that I had a brain that was actually functional. He always made me want to rise to any challenge. Same with Ms. Samara, my homeroom teacher. And my English teacher, Mrs. Hawkes, urged me to take her creative writing class. I figured, "What the hell, sounds easy!" But it wasn't—at first anyway. One day, after class, she took me aside and said, "You know, I always hear you telling funny stories to your friends in class. You should write down some of those stories and we can make that your homework assignment." Hey, it sounded better than poetry!

So I gave it a try and—amazingly—it turned out to be the first time I ever did homework where I wasn't waiting for Ricky Nelson to come on TV. I actually enjoyed it. I'd spend hours writing a story (usually about something stupid that happened at school), reading it to myself, crossing out things that weren't funny. I'd go four or five drafts, then hand it in. Suddenly, it was fun to go to class and read my funny story—and, best of all, to get some laughs. I was always grateful to Mrs. Hawkes for that.

Another teacher who made a huge impression on me was Mr. Walsh. For whatever reason, he was always assigned to oversee detention duty in the library. And since I was *always* in detention, we'd sit together almost every day. Mr. Walsh was one of those guys who would laugh at anything. Tell him the simplest joke and he'd break up. Everything was *hilarious* to this man. So I'd have new stories for him all the time. One day he said to me, "Why don't you think about going into show business?"

This was a new revelation. The idea never occurred to me. I didn't know anyone in the business. The closest thing was an eighth-grade teacher named Mr. Duncan, who did magic tricks at student assemblies. And that was *unbelievable!* Someone we knew could actually *entertain* people! When you grow up in a small town like Andover, show business is the furthest thing from being a career option.

But Mr. Walsh's words ignited something in me. I began telling people that I wanted to one day become a comedian.

JOHN McCAIN
United States Senator
born: 1936

❓WHY JOHN

Because as the U.S. senator from Arizona and a one-time presidential candidate, John McCain devotes his life to public service.

Because he learned firsthand about human suffering during the Vietnam War when his plane was shot down and he was held prisoner-of-war in Hanoi for five and a half years, much of that time in solitary confinement.

Because Captain John McCain served in the navy for twenty-two years before retiring in 1981.

In boarding school, John McCain was prone to collecting detention slips. He served his time cleaning up the campus and teachers' yards. The upside of getting in trouble was the time spent with the great Mr. Ravenel, a teacher who was a major influence in McCain's life.

JOHN'S STORY:

Were William B. Ravenel the only person I remember from high school, I would credit those days as among the best of my life. Mr. Ravenel headed the English department at

EHS, and he coached the junior varsity football team, on which I played. . . .

. . . Demerits required the offender to march ceaselessly around the long circle drive in the front of the school or to tend the yard of a master's house. It was my good fortune to have received, for many transgressions, assignment to work in Mr. Ravenel's yard. Perhaps the school authorities knew they were doing me a favor—knew that Mr. Ravenel was best able to repair the all too evident flaws in my character.

I don't know if it was their benevolence or providence that brought me to his attention. Neither do I understand why it was that Mr. Ravenel took such an interest in me, seeing in me something that few others did. But that he did take an interest in me was apparent to all. . . .

I discussed all manner of subjects with him, from sports to the stories of Somerset Maugham, from his combat experiences to my future. He was one of the few people at school to whom I confided that I was bound for the Academy and a Navy career, and to whom I confessed my reservations about my destiny.

In the fall of my senior year, a member of the junior varsity football team had broken training and been found out. I cannot recall the exact nature of the offense, but it was serious enough to merit his expulsion from the team. Mr. Ravenel called a team meeting, and most of the players argued that the accused be dropped from the team. I stood and offered the only argument for a less severe punishment.

The student in question had, in fact, broken training. But unlike the rest of us, he had chosen at the start of the year not to sign a pledge promising to abide by the training rules faithfully. Had he signed the pledge, he would have been expelled from school, because violating the pledge constituted an honor offense. Had he signed it, I wouldn't have defended him. But he had not. Moreover, he had not been caught breaking training, but had confessed the offense and expressed his remorse freely, without fear of discovery. I thought his behavior was no less honorable than that of a student who signed the pledge and adhered to its provisions. . . .

At the start, most of my teammates wanted to hang the guy. But I argued that he had made a mistake that he sincerely regretted, and, uncoerced, had admitted the infraction. His behavior warranted no further disciplinary action. As I talked, I noticed Mr. Ravenel nodding his head. When some of the other guys started to come around to my point of view, Mr. Ravenel closed the discussion by voicing support for my judgment. The team then voted to drop the matter.

After the meeting broke up, Mr. Ravenel approached me and shook my hand. With relief evident in his voice, he told me we had done the right thing, and thanked me for my efforts. He allowed that before the meeting he had been anxious about its outcome. He had hoped the matter would be resolved as it had been, but was uncertain it would. Still, he had not wanted to be the one who argued for exoneration; he wanted the decision to be ours and not his. He said he was proud of me.

HECTOR ELIZONDO

Actor

born: 1936

? WHY HECTOR

Because Hector Elizondo is the man you've seen again and again playing the good guy, the crook, the chauffeur, the father, in his movies and Broadway shows. He's appeared in *The Princess Diaries* and *Tortilla Soup* and in many Arthur Miller plays.

Hector Elizondo had a tough guy mentality but lacked the build to match it. He needed street smarts and defensive moves to survive in his New York neighborhood. A teacher, aware of Hector's struggle, encouraged him to beef up his body and mind. It turned out to be a power-packed suggestion. Hector not only became well read, he became one of the best baseball players in the city.

HECTOR'S STORY:

I'm from the streets of New York, a tough neighborhood that was also rich in music and art, though I didn't realize it until I left. I was not a strong kid. I was skinny and not very assertive or aggressive. I was on this side of being a mama's boy and that was always a disappointment to my dad, and also not a good thing to be in my neighborhood.

One of my great mentors was Mr. Mortimer Engle. I'll never forget him. He was a vertically challenged gentleman with a big barrel chest who stood straight as a ramrod. He had a great nose and quite a presence despite his height. We didn't think of him as short because he didn't think of himself that way. He was our English teacher and he was very cultured and a great ex-athlete—a wrestler and a boxer and also a basket-ball player in spite of his height. He was the first fellow to nudge me toward reading books. He also encouraged me to reinvent myself physically because he sensed that I would not thrive in my neighborhood being as skinny as I was.

Junior high school was an important time in my adolescence. I was twelve years old, had an interest in athletics, and was coordinated but quite weak. So my real transition began when Mortimer Engle took an interest in me and would not let me off the hook. He gave me these pep talks. He'd never put his arm around you unless he was making a point, kind of like Vince Lombardi of the Green Bay Packers. Mr. Engle also loved literature and turned me on to great authors like Jack London, Robert Louis Stevenson, and Edgar Allan Poe. He was always encouraging me not to waste my life. He used to say, "You only have so much of it and what you bring into your mind goes right to your heart and your heart forms who you are." Something happened to me. This big change occurred. I decided I wanted to make the baseball team and so I started to exercise, to build muscle and gain weight.

JAMES CAMERON

Film Director, Producer, Writer

born: 1954

❓WHY JAMES

Because he's the special-effects king, creator, and mastermind behind the action films *Terminator, Aliens, True Lies, The Abyss,* and *Titanic*.

Because James Cameron wowed the world with *Titanic*, which garnered eleven Academy Awards and earned more money than any other movie in the history of filmmaking.

The young James Cameron was always comfortable in his own shoes, but like all people, he thrived on an encouraging compliment. When he least expected it, a teacher paid him praise for his talents. Cameron remembered how special he felt and how empowered he felt to continue with his goals.

JAMES'S STORY:

I remember very clearly doing some testing at our school. There was a biology teacher who I really liked, and he also started the theater arts program. He just bootstrapped it one day, and said, "Hey, we need to be doing theater." There was a small group of kids that jumped in on that. We just volunteered, did all the work after hours, set up the stage, set up the lighting and did all that stuff, wrote plays, put them on, and all that crazy stuff. So he was busy empowering the entire group, but I remember one day, he came up to me in the hall and said, "I know you. You've been in my class twice over the last couple of years. I've looked at your scores, and I just want you to know that you fall into a category where we believe you have unlimited potential." It was simultaneously a really big boost but also terrifying, because I thought, "How do I translate that?" And whether that was true or not, it was a good thing to hear. I think teachers should just say that to every kid.

EARVIN "MAGIC" JOHNSON

Former Professional Basketball Player, Businessman

born: 1959

 WHY EARVIN

Because he's the pro-ball, All-Star, Olympic athlete who wowed fans by scoring when they thought he would pass and passing when they thought he would score.

Because as the point guard and forward for the Los Angeles Lakers for thirteen seasons, he helped his team bring home five NBA Championships, was voted MVP, and played in twelve All-Star tournaments.

Because after being infected with HIV, Magic retired from basketball and redefined himself as a business-man who focuses on revitalizing neglected communities and providing quality film and television entertainment to all.

Because he created the Magic Johnson Foundation, dedicated to serve the educational, health, and social needs of urban youth. That's why they call him Magic.

Magic Johnson's teacher Greta Dart had high standards for him. She knew he had talent on the basketball court but also knew he had to study to stay in school. Her concern was for Earvin Johnson the whole person and her influence made him realize that there was more to life than just sports.

EARVIN'S STORY:

I don't know exactly when I understood that basketball was more than just a game for me, or when the outside world started to matter, but I was probably around ten. My fifth-grade teacher, Greta Dart, and her husband, Jim, played a role in my growing up that was second only to my parents'. Outside of my family, they were the most important adults in my life. And for all that's happened since, we're still close.

Aside from everything else they taught me in the classroom, on the court, and in their home, they were also my first (and closest) white friends. Getting to know the Darts allowed me to start feeling comfortable with white people. For many black kids in America, that just doesn't happen. . . .

My friendship with Mrs. Dart almost ended when she and I got into an argument that was one of the real tests of my childhood. I was playing in a Saturday-morning basketball league, and our championship game was scheduled for the weekend. A few days earlier I had come to school without my homework. Mrs. Dart told me to stay after class so I could do it.

"I can't," I said. "We've got a practice."

"I'm sorry, Earvin, but you've got to do this assignment."

"But we've got our big game on Saturday."

"I know. But if you don't finish the assignment, you won't be able to play."

"You can't make me miss that game!" I said. Technically, I might have been right. But I never should have said that. Now the two of us were in a contest of wills. When I continued to refuse to do the assignment, Mrs. Dart told the coach that I couldn't play. She also called my parents to tell them what happened, so now I was in double trouble.

I did everything I could to smooth things over. I called Mrs. Dart at home. I begged her to change her mind. I went to see her after school. "You don't understand," I said. "This is the league championship. The team needs me. I can do the assignment next week."

"No," she said again. "Unless you finish the assignment before the game, you can't play."

I was pretty sure she was bluffing, and I showed up at the game anyway. When the coach told me I couldn't play, I was furious. I was even more angry as I sat on the bench and watched our team lose for the first time all season. We lost that game by one point.

I cried that day, and I vowed that I'd never speak to Mrs. Dart again. I stayed angry at her for weeks. I still don't fully understand why, but after my anger wore off, Mrs. Dart and I became even closer. Maybe I respected her for following through on her threat. Or maybe I was secretly proud that she saw me as more than just an athlete, that she expected me to be a good student, too.

CHAPTER 6

YOU'VE GOT THE POWER

... to Persevere

THE VOICE

There is a voice inside of you
That whispers all day long,
"I feel that this is right for me,
I know that *this* is wrong."
No teacher, preacher, parent, friend
Or wise man can decide
What's right for you—just listen to
The voice that speaks inside.

—SHEL SILVERSTEIN

That's right. It's inside you and the time is now to persevere and make your dreams a reality. Sound simple? It is when you approach it with the right attitude. You've got the hunger and passion to do what you love. It could be winning a school competition or a state championship.

It could be giving your best performance in a Shakespeare festival or becoming an Eagle Scout. Think of pursuing your passion in terms of setting goals. Think how you are going to get there and before you know it—you are in the driver's seat, controlling your destiny. You are living large, chasing down your dreams, reaching your goals. When you persevere . . . you've got the power!

Ah, yes, and be prepared because annoying obstacles will get in your way. Some people will tell you it's not a good idea. There's not enough time for practice and homework, too. You can't afford the equipment or dues. There's always an obstacle to block you, keep you from achieving your goals. If you get derailed, hunker down and create a smaller set of goals to get you back on track. Debate those who question your dream. Find the time to practice. Take a part-time job to help pay for the things you need. There's always a way. When you persevere, you are tuned into the word "yes" not "no."

The men in this chapter did not let outside noise distract them. Christopher Reeve got "hooked" hearing the roar of applause after his first performance. Tupac

Shakur said, "Where there's a will, there's a way." Basketball consumed Magic Johnson's thoughts—he had to play.

Move forward. Feed your passion. Make history. You are in control and only you know how you really feel. So listen to your voice. Have fun. *Persevere!*

CHUCK LEAVELL

Rock and Roll Musician, Tree Farmer

born: 1952

? WHY CHUCK

Because when he's not playing keyboard for the Rolling Stones, he's a successful tree farmer in Georgia.

Because Chuck Leavell's talents have been tapped by Eric Clapton, the Black Crowes, George Harrison, the Indigo Girls, Blues Traveler, and many more.

Once Chuck Leavell made the decision to be a musician, he went for it, and that meant taking risks, selling himself. Armed with a pleasing Southern manner, Leavell pushed the envelope by introducing himself to already established musicians. He figured the worst that could happen was hearing the word "no." If he did, he just knocked on the next door. When he was at the ripe old age of twenty, Leavell's persistence nudged a door open, and by walking through it, he became a member of the Allman Brothers Band. The rest, as they say, is history.

CHUCK'S STORY:

I think you make your own luck by understanding what opportunities are there and by moving on them, taking action, and trying to make things happen. When I was a young musician in Alabama and trying to play with better musicians so I could advance my career, I went to a place called Mussel Shoals, where the well-respected studios were and still are today. At the time, it was a real hotbed of activity for music, not only in the South, but in the whole country.

I would literally stand outside the doors of clubs and when artists like Leon Russell, Joe Cocker, and others who were recording inside took a break, I'd walk in and introduce myself. I'd be polite, not pushy, and try to find the right moment to play the piano, hoping someone would hear me.

That served me very well, not just at Mussel Shoals, but anywhere I thought the good bands were playing. I'd be polite and get backstage somehow in hopes of meeting someone. Or I'd show up early when I knew the band would be doing a sound check or setting up equipment, always with the hope of meeting someone who could help me move my career forward.

CHRIS KLUG

Professional Snowboarder

born: 1972

 WHY CHRIS

Because national- and world-champ snowboarder Chris Klug says, "Bring on the speed." He's driven by the love of the sport. His positive attitude brings him home endless trophies and prize money.

Because after suffering from a condition called primary sclerosing cholangitis, Klug got a second chance on life after undergoing liver transplant surgery in 2000.

Because two years after the transplant, he competed at the 2002 Olympics in Park City and brought home the bronze medal.

Because he's committed to educating people about the importance of organ donation in saving lives.

For Chris Klug, snowboarding isn't a sport, it's a passion, a lifestyle, a state of mind. Growing up in Bend, Oregon, gave this snowboarder access to the slopes at a very young age. In no time, he caught the bug. He quickly adopted his parents' "don't give up" attitude that has served him well on and off the slopes. After undergoing a liver transplant, competing head-to-head in a parallel giant slalom at the World Cup seemed easy. A master of perseverance, Klug is grateful for the opportunity to just keep trying.

CHRIS'S STORY:

I loved junior high and high school. Any free time I had, I was snowboarding. I was also very involved in school athletics and played quarterback on the high school football team. I loved playing for my school, and it is one of my greatest memories.

Though I remember high school offering some challenges, the tough ones came once I graduated. I was confused and not at all sure what I wanted to do. My true love was snowboarding, but it was such a new sport at the time. There was no international level to compete at and certainly no Olympic platform. It was in a state of evolution, and though I wanted to dedicate myself to competing, it was a leap of faith for me. What helped was that I just sensed a future there. It's where my heart was and what I loved doing, so I said no to some college-scholarship opportunities to play football. I wanted to snowboard. I just didn't want to give it up.

It was a risky decision to make because there was

no guaranteed future in snowboarding, but it's what I loved, so I made that leap. My attitude was, this is what I was going to do and if it worked out, cool. If not, I'd take another route and go back to school.

DANNY VILLANUEVA

Former Professional Football Player, Business Executive, Philanthropist

born: 1937

 ## WHY DANNY

Because he was the placekicker for the Los Angeles Rams from 1960 to 1964 and for the Dallas Cowboys from 1965 to 1967, and still holds several NFL kicking records.

Because during his playing years, Danny Villanueva worked part-time as a news director at KMEX-TV in Los Angeles. Moving up the corporate ladder, he became general manager and then president, turning KMEX into the most profitable Spanish-speaking television station in the United States.

Because his involvement with the Spanish-language television networks Univision and Telemundo changed the face of Spanish television.

Because Villanueva is passionate about young people and works with several nonprofits aimed at helping them stay in school.

Danny Villanueva got through football season on sheer gumption. Always prepared to give it his best kick, he also prepared a backup plan for his future, like teaching English. But Danny made it to the pros, and at that time, he was the only Latino playing in the NFL.

DANNY'S STORY:

As a student at Calexico High School, I took a good look at myself in the mirror. I was short, fat, slow. I would never be able to compete in basketball. My competitive advantages were my legs. I could learn to kick a football instead. I realized that if I worked really hard, I could be a pretty good kicker. I was determined that no one would ever outwork me. I made myself into a kicker because that was my ticket. I simply willed it.

People told me, "You are just a good little high school player, but you are not good enough to play at the college level." Did they have to say *little?* In response, I worked and worked and worked. I played football at New Mexico Sate University, where I majored in English, Spanish, and journalism and ran the campus newspaper. I did not see professional football as an option in my future, so I decided to be an English teacher.

During my senior year, I made an exceptionally long kick against the University of New Mexico. Chuck Benedict, a scout for the Rams, was in the stands. Later, I was told that he wrote my name among his notes. Before spring training, the Rams knew they needed a kicker. Chuck looked up my name in his notebook and called the university. They gave him the number at Las Cruces, New Mexico, where I was doing my student teaching.

I got a note from the school office saying I had a call from Bob Waterfield of the Rams, and I made some sort of wisecrack. The office staff said, "This is for real, Danny. You have a call waiting." Despite all my hard work in college, the NFL had never been interested in me. Now I had an offer to try out for the Rams.

CHRISTOPHER REEVE

Actor, Political Activist

born: 1952

? WHY CHRISTOPHER

Because he will go down in history as playing Superman on the big screen and being a superhero to all his fans, while rehabilitating after a life-altering fall from his horse in 1995 that left him paralyzed.

Because he founded the Christopher Reeve Paralysis Foundation, a leader in finding a cure for paralysis and in bettering the lives of the physically challenged.

Because Christopher Reeve is a hero who found the strength to pursue and endure despite overwhelming obstacles.

The theater grounded Christopher Reeve. It was comfortable, a safe haven from his unstable home life. He could be himself when working on the set and pretend to be someone else when acting onstage. He loved the theater world and the affirmation he received onstage. Mastering a goal and having fun doing it painted a promising future for Reeve.

CHRISTOPHER'S STORY:

One day in the spring of 1962, when I was nine, somebody came over to Princeton Country Day (PCD) from the Princeton Savoyards, an amateur group that put on Gilbert and Sullivan operettas once or twice a year. She asked if any of us could sing and would like to try out for a production of *The Yeomen of the Guard.* I shot up my hand and went for the tryout. I was cast with grown-ups over at McCarter Theater, the big thousand-seat theater that had been built in the twenties to house productions of the Princeton Triangle Club. I was given the small part of a townsperson. It was my first time onstage, and it was intoxicating.

It was one thing to be a good student-athlete, but acting was even better. I even got to miss school for rehearsals. McCarter had a state-sponsored program of student matinees, usually at 10:30 in the morning or 2:30 in the afternoon. I would get to pack up my books and walk out of the classroom for a performance. I was special.

Then I started to act at PCD. When I was eleven or twelve, we put on a production of Agatha Christie's *Witness for the Prosecution,* and, of course, all the parts were played by boys. I was cast as Janet Mackenzie, the sixty-five-year-old housekeeper in the mansion where the murders take place. I was outfitted with a gray wig and a dowdy Scottish tweed housekeeper's suit. At one point in the play, Janet Mackenzie fiercely defends her actions, insisting that she's not guilty. On opening night, as I was finishing a heated exchange from the witness box, I got applause from the audience. Right in the middle of the first act. It went straight to my head, and I thought, this is wonderful.

I found every excuse I could to get down to the theater. Even before they started casting me in plays, I went down and wired dressing-room speakers for sound and worked on the light board.

Before long I was cast in small parts with the professional repertory company at McCarter. It felt like a family. I was part of a group of people who worked together every day on projects they believed in. All the horses were pulling the wagon in the same direction, toward opening night. And during the rehearsal process the excitement grew as a play started to jell. I loved the whole atmosphere. No strife, no tension here, at least none that I could see. I behaved myself and tried hard, and the adults liked me. Right there was the beginning of a way to escape the conflicting feelings I had about my two families. I'm sure that's why I became an actor.

ANSEL ADAMS
Photographer, Conservationist
1902-1984

? WHY ANSEL

Because he was the master photographer of the West. Ansel Adams's legendary black-and-white photos of Yosemite National Park and other natural landscapes offer visions of beauty so grand, they have become the standard by which all other nature photos are judged.

Because as a board member of the Sierra Club for nearly forty years, Adams focused on working with the government to preserve national parks.

Because America claimed Ansel Adams as its own national treasure by awarding him the prestigious National Medal of Freedom, the nation's highest civil honor.

It was Ansel Adams's idea to take a family trip to Yosemite National Park in California. The year was 1916. Carrying his first camera, a Kodak Box Brownie, a gift given by his parents, Ansel hadn't planned on feeling such exhilaration once he entered the park. At the time, he was devoted to piano and had hopes of becoming a professional musician, but that trip to Yosemite changed his course. Capturing Yosemite's stunning beauty in his camera lens became his quest; perfecting camera skills, his goal. From that moment on, he knew he would be a photographer just as he knew the natural wonders of Yosemite National Park would be his canvas.

ANSEL'S STORY:

How different my life would have been if it were not for these early hikes in the Sierra—if I had not experienced that memorable first trip to Yosemite—if I had not been raised by the ocean—if, if, if! Everything I have done or felt has been in some way influenced by the impact of the Natural Scene.

It is easy to recount that I camped many times at Merced Lake, but it is difficult to explain the magic: to lie in a small recess of the granite matrix of the Sierra and watch the progress of dusk to night, the incredible brilliance of the stars, the waning of the glittering sky into dawn, and the following sunrise on the peaks and domes around me. And always that cool dawn wind that I believe to be the prime benediction of the Sierra. These qualities to which I still deeply respond were distilled into my pictures over the decades. I knew my destiny when I first experienced Yosemite.

At this point I was not a professional or creative photographer, but an ardent hobbyist, if that term can be applied to a curious youth who wanted to try everything within reach. Though I was still deeply immersed in music, during the decade of the twenties, photography and hiking were my beloved diversions. From my music studies, I applied the axiom of "practice makes perfect" to my photography. Mastering the craft of photography came through years of continued work, as did the ability to make images of personal expression. Step by inevitable step, the intuitive process slowly became part of my picture making.

EARVIN "MAGIC" JOHNSON

Former Professional Basketball Player, Businessman

born: 1959

? WHY EARVIN

Because he's the pro-ball, All-Star, Olympic athlete who wowed fans by scoring when they thought he would pass and passing when they thought he would score.

Because as the point guard and forward for the Los Angeles Lakers for thirteen seasons, he helped his team bring home five NBA Championships, was voted MVP, and played in twelve All-Star tournaments.

Because after being infected with HIV, Magic retired from basketball and redefined himself as a businessman who focuses on revitalizing neglected communities and providing quality film and television entertainment to all.

Because he created the Magic Johnson Foundation, dedicated to serve the educational, health, and social needs of urban youth. That's why they call him Magic.

Magic Johnson couldn't help himself. He always made time for basketball. And like anything in life, the more you work at it, the better you become. Magic is the Man—whether slipping a sly behind-the-back pass or dunking before the buzzer sounds, Magic's got the gift. Did he sit and *think* about playing hoops when he was a boy? No—he played day and night, rain or shine.

EARVIN'S STORY:

No matter what else I was doing, I always had a basketball in my hand. If I was running an errand for my mother, I'd dribble on the way to the store. Just to make it interesting, I'd alternate right hand and left, block by block.

I remember waking up when it was still dark outside and wanting to play ball so badly that I'd just lie there, looking out the window, waiting for daybreak. If it was too early to go to the schoolyard, I'd dribble on the street. I'd run around the parked cars and pretend they were players on the other team. All up and down Middle Street people used to open their windows and yell at me for waking them up. But I couldn't help it. The game was just in me.

Mom had strict rules about playing ball in the house,

and I knew she meant business. So on rainy days I would make a special indoor basketball by rolling up some of my father's socks. For the basket, I'd take a pencil and draw a little box high on the wall. Sometimes I played with my sisters, or my brother Larry. But usually I played alone, shooting into the box on the wall or a trash can or making foul shots into a laundry basket at the top of the stairs. One way or another, I had to play.

NEIL LEIFER
Photojournalist
born: 1942

? WHY NEIL

Because so many famous sports photos have been taken by Neil Leifer.

Because since 1960, over 200 of his images have graced the covers of *Sports Illustrated, Time,* and *People* magazines, making him the most published photojournalist in Time, Inc., history.

Because for fifteen Olympic Games, every gold-medal winner has been the focus of Leifer's lens.

Make photo history by spending the day with the president of the United States. Work with Olympic champions and place their photos on the cover of *Time* and *Sports Illustrated* magazines. Go to sea on the battleship *New Jersey* and document sailors' lives in photos. Sit ringside with Muhammad Ali and take his most famous photo. Neil Leifer carved out these experiences for himself because he loved taking pictures. The more he took, the better he got. The more he traveled, the more he learned. Neil walked the talk and persevered.

NEIL'S STORY:

I had a lot of parental pressure. My parents thought that a bright young Jewish boy from the Lower East Side should become a doctor or a lawyer—not a photographer. They worked hard to give me opportunities, especially when they saw I had the aptitude and intelligence. They wondered how I was going to make a living when I grew up, but kids don't think about that. It was the furthest thought from my mind.

My dad believed photography was a rich man's hobby and wondered when I was going to grow up and go back to school, which I ultimately did.

I don't want to say that I went against my parents, but I think when a kid has a passion and it's something they really want to do, they've got to make the effort to do it. You can't catch up later on. I'm sure I could have followed my parents' advice and gone on to college and done something that perhaps I would have had success at, but I doubt I would have been as happy. I don't believe I would have had as satisfying a career doing something that I really didn't love doing.

I am living proof that this is a country where you can do or be anything. I certainly didn't have a family that provided me with things that could have made it easy for me to pursue a profession. But once I had a dream and once I saw what photography could do for me, I wanted to travel the world and see things. I've often been quoted as saying, "My camera was my passport to the world."

TUPAC Musician, Poet
SHAKUR 1971–1996

❓ WHY TUPAC

Because 2Pac still rules. Even after his death from a gunshot wound at age twenty-five, the stories of heartbreak, ambition, and passion told in the music of this controversial and introspective street poet still appeal to all races.

Tupac Shakur held on to hope. Sometimes it was all he had. Hope that promised dreams of a better life.

When faced with daunting pressures from school or family, remembering that tomorrow is another day helps. It helped Tupac. Hope always found a way to rear its head and say, "Where there is a will . . ."

WHERE THERE IS A WILL . . .

When there is a will
there is a way
2 search and discover
a better day
Where a positive heart
Is all you need
2 Rise Beyond
and succeed

Where young minds grow
And respect each other
Based on their Deeds
And not their color

When times R dim
say as I say
"Where there is a will
There is a way!"

CHAPTER 7

FINAL WORDS

Some Wise Advice

SUCCESS . . .

To laugh often and much; to win the respect of intelligent people; to appreciate beauty; to find the best in others; to leave the world a bit better, whether by a healthy child, a garden patch, or a redeemed social condition; to know even one life has breathed easier because you have lived. This is to have succeeded.

—RALPH WALDO EMERSON

We all show up at the table of life with our own strengths and weaknesses. That's why we need to borrow from and give to one another. Sharing life experiences is how we learn.

Some life experiences deliver lessons at a time

when we are much too young to cope emotionally. The death of a parent catapults a young person into a world that most of us don't have to experience until later on in adulthood. Some learn at fifty what others learned in college.

Looking back at that time when they were your age, the men in this chapter shared thoughts about what worked and what didn't. The following list offers the high points of what they had to say:

- This, too, will pass.
- Follow your dreams, not your parents' dream.
- Read as much as you can.
- Don't take yourself too seriously.
- Respect yourself.
- Respect the environment.
- Don't give up.
- Learn from your mistakes.
- Don't compare.

They hoped that by taking these thoughts into account, you might be spared a little pain. Isn't that reason enough to continue reading?

Quite possibly, you've heard it all before, but consider this: There could be a reason why the same wise words get repeated over and over. They might just be tried and true.

The famous men profiled in *The Boldness of Boys* were eager to offer words of advice. After reading what they had to say, you might realize that you're already on your way to making the world a better place.

DAVE BARRY
Humor Columnist

born: 1947

? WHY DAVE

Because Dave Barry writes a newspaper column about ordinary events that makes readers laugh out loud at the absurdities of life.

Because Barry's Pulitzer Prize–winning humor column is syndicated nationally in over 500 newspapers.

Because he still wonders how that happened.

Because he has also written twenty-four books, including *Big Trouble*, which was made into a motion picture.

Laugh it off and lighten up. Making jokes was Dave Barry's tactic for survival. No matter how old you are, Barry believes humor is the best antidote when life gets too complicated.

DAVE'S ADVICE:

Don't take anything that happens while you're a teenager too seriously. It's so easy to think that what's going on now is all that's *ever* going to happen to you—that this is really the way the world works—but it's just not true. At my age now, even though I still haven't figured out how it all works, coping with the unknown is so much easier than it ever was in junior high!

KELLY SLATER
World Champion Surfer

born: 1972

❓ WHY KELLY

Because he's number one, the man to beat. No one compares to this winner of six surfing world titles.

Because he took time off in 1990 to get even smarter and now he's back on the board, riding waves, winning competitions, with his new thirty-year-old perspective.

Kelly Slater never stops learning. His constant thirst for knowledge is why his approach to the sport of surfing is always evolving. He loves to study the success of other people and then apply those lessons to his own life. His advice is simple: Be in the moment, concentrate, and you'll find your own style.

KELLY'S ADVICE:

I think everyone has their own unique approach. People have different opinions and different things that they find interesting and attractive and exciting. Everyone has something unique to offer. I always felt like you should take the things you like from other people, whether it is a personality trait or the way they do something or the way a person speaks. The people around us influence us on all those levels. In surfing, I might take one guy's bottom turn or the way another guy rides a wave or the way someone tube rides. Incorporating into my own approach techniques I observe in other surfers is how I keep learning.

It's really important to feel what you're doing, to get lost in it. You should spend your life following what you love to do. Be consumed; whether it's art, business, sports, whatever it is, do what you love to do most. I've always felt strongly that people shouldn't spend their lives complaining. When you become as good at something as you can be, your instincts will tell you where to take it next.

GLEN BALLARD
Songwriter, Producer
born: 1953

 **WHY GLEN**

Because this five-time Grammy Award winner cowrote and produced Alanis Morissette's album *Jagged Little Pill*.

Because Glen Ballard has written and produced songs for Michael Jackson, Shelby Lynne, Van Halen, Dave Matthews Band, Aerosmith, and many others.

Because as the music industry's most sought-after writer and producer, Ballard's number one goal is helping musicians realize their artistic vision.

Glen Ballard listened to his own heart. Instead of accepting a law school scholarship, he left Mississippi and headed west to begin a career in music. It worked because Glen made it happen. Music burned in his soul. His commitment was to find a way to express it.

GLEN'S ADVICE:

Always try to educate yourself and become better at whatever it is that you want to do. There's just no substitute for making a commitment to something. I see a lot of young people who don't have the good fortune to know what it is they want to do. I think it's so important to read and study about what interests you. I also encourage young people not to look for shortcuts, because there are none. Anyone who is successful got there through effort and hard work. Get good at what you do. Often I get submissions of songs from people who think if they just get their song into the right hands, it'll be a hit. I always say if something is truly good, people will be beating down your door. Sure, you hear stories about how someone became a "star" overnight, but most of the time, those stars have prepared for years for that opportunity.

It takes a lot of hard work to get what you want. I know this is the sort of thing people don't really want to hear, but being fulfilled as a human being is always the result of hard work. If you never challenge yourself to achieve goals, then you can't appreciate what it's like to reach them.

If you love movies, watch every movie you can watch and learn the film vocabulary. If you want to be a writer, read, read, read. Read the best and worst writers. Read everything you can get your hands on. The best way to broaden your own perspective is to learn from other people's experiences. And be realistic. If you are five feet four inches and you love basketball, you won't go pro but that doesn't mean you can't enjoy the game. If it's music you love, but you can't master an instrument, consider composing and arranging songs. There's always an avenue to get you where you want to go. Look for it.

DANNY VILLANUEVA

Former Professional Football Player, Business Executive, Philanthropist

born: 1937

? WHY DANNY

Because he was the placekicker for the Los Angeles Rams from 1960 to 1964 and for the Dallas Cowboys from 1965 to 1967, and still holds several NFL kicking records.

Because during his playing years, Danny Villanueva worked part-time as a news director at KMEX-TV in Los Angeles. Moving up the corporate ladder, he became general manager and then president, turning KMEX into the most profitable Spanish-speaking television station in the United States.

Because his involvement with the Spanish-language television networks Univision and Telemundo changed the face of Spanish television.

Because Villanueva is passionate about young people and works with several nonprofits aimed at helping them stay in school.

Danny Villanueva believes giving back to the community builds character, a belief taught by his parents. He has created mentoring programs that help high school students get into college and that require those students to help younger ones get into junior high. Pass along the good stuff and you will be remembered for making a difference in someone's life.

DANNY'S ADVICE:

A theory that I've taken to heart is that character is not a gift. Character is a victory. We work on it; we seek it. When our time comes, we hope people will look at our life and say, "There stood a person with character."

Nobody's born with character. You work at developing it so that when the end is here and we are judged, the world will say, "He was a man of character. He made a difference." That to me is the ultimate victory in life.

MARTIN RICHARDS
Broadway and Film Producer
born: 1932

❓ WHY MARTIN

Because Martin Richards has the magic touch. A producer extraordinaire of stage and screen, his most recent mega Broadway play and film production of *Chicago* was nominated for eleven Tony Awards and won six Academy Awards.

FINAL WORDS

Because as head of the film and theatrical company, the Producer's Circle, he has produced runaway hits on stage, including *On the Twentieth Century, Sweeney Todd, The Will Rogers Follies,* and *La Cage Aux Folles,* all of which earned numerous awards. His films include *The Shining, The Boys from Brazil,* and *Fort Apache, the Bronx.*

Because Martin Richards doesn't just produce great entertainment, he produces much goodwill. He has cofounded a medical center for organ transplantation and research and a nonprofit organization for abused children, and he sits on many boards supporting the arts culture in New York City.

Martin Richards Klein's doting grandmother always called out to him in one breath "Martin Richards." Named after both sides of his family, he dropped the "Klein" once he began singing professionally. His mother wanted him to become an architect like his uncles but Richards had other plans. Surrounded by an extended family that became his first audience, he always felt like the star he dreamed of becoming. His advice to young people is simple: Give yourself time to develop your dream. Knowing when to continue and when to quit is part of the journey.

MARTIN'S ADVICE:

Don't let anyone ever talk you out of your dream. Just know that you have to work for your dream to come true. It doesn't just happen. If you say you want to be an actor or a singer or a rock star or an advertising whiz, you have to work for it. Nothing comes free. Beyond that, no matter how many lucky breaks you might get, I believe getting the best education possible is a key ingredient. It enhances your opportunities by opening up more avenues to explore within and beyond whatever you set your sights on.

And whatever you do, don't give yourself a time limit. Everyone I know in the business, including myself, tries to do this and it shouldn't be. Let it play out. If you have to quit, you'll just know when it's time. And if you stick to it and love what you do, there is no greater gift you can give yourself than the opportunity to realize your dream.

ROBERT BALLARD
Explorer, Oceanographer
born: 1942

❓ WHY ROBERT

Because as president of the Institute for Exploration in Mystic, Connecticut, Robert Ballard and his team located the *Titanic* in 1985.

Because the interest in the *Titanic* from children was so overwhelming, he created the Jason Project, an educational organization that teaches kids about his expeditions through live video-feeds beamed over the Internet to more than 200,000 million students.

Because he's made over 100 deep-sea expeditions, discovering other shipwrecks like the *Bismarck,* the *Yorktown,* the *Lusitania,* and the famous *PT-109* from World War II.

Because Ballard believes in curating his discoveries and leaving everything as he and his team found it.

Because he's still learning and teaching others at the University of Rhode Island Graduate, School of Oceanography.

Robert Ballard has always tried to embrace his passion and finds himself frustrated with people who don't or won't pursue theirs. This feeling is no doubt influenced by having grown up with a handicapped sister who didn't have as many opportunities. He has always been determined not to squander his good fortune.

ROBERT'S ADVICE:

The only true advice I have for boys and girls is don't live your mom's dream or your dad's dream or your teacher's dream. Don't let anyone talk you into anything. Follow your passion.

Now, initially your passion may seem silly because it manifests itself in perhaps a silly way. My passion was to be Captain Nemo when I was a child. Silly, maybe, but it was enough to fuel me even when I met obstacles. Consider passion to be your driving engine—the force that gets you through thick and thin. For sure, you're going to get knocked down. Your passion will get you back up again. Your mind is useful and you need to train it, so think of it as a tool, but your passion is the essence of you.

JAMES CAMERON
Film Director, Producer, Writer
born: 1954

? WHY JAMES

Because he's the special-effects king, creator, and mastermind behind the action films *Terminator, Aliens, True Lies, The Abyss,* and *Titanic.*

Because James Cameron wowed the world with *Titanic,* which garnered eleven Academy Awards and earned more money than any other movie in the history of filmmaking.

To be interested is to be interesting and therein lies the essence of James Cameron. He's fascinated with how things work and loves surprising his movie audiences with outrageous special effects. As a kid, James's imagination steered the boat. Living up to his word guided him to where he is today.

JAMES'S ADVICE:

Live with honor. That's the most important advice I can offer: Honor your word. I think so many people look for shortcuts and rationalizations for why they did something that they knew was wrong. If you make the old-fashioned values of honor and duty a priority, good things will come back to you. A lot of this may sound corny, but it's what I've lived by. I work in a field where the only people who seem to be getting rich are the attorneys, and that's because so many people don't keep their word, so everyone has to have a six-hundred-page contract to seal the deal. Almost everything I've done has essentially been on a handshake. People know that even if it costs me hundreds of thousands or even millions of dollars, I'll honor my word. It's also incumbent on them to do that as well.

The other thing that boys growing into men should learn is how to treat women. Keep your libido in check and treat them with respect. It's a very simple thing.

JEAN-MICHEL COUSTEAU

Explorer, Environmentalist, Educator, Film Producer

born: 1938

 WHY JEAN-MICHEL

Because as the son of world-famous ocean explorer Jacques Cousteau, he takes seriously his responsibility to continue his father's pioneering work in ocean exploration.

Because as the founder of Ocean Futures Society, Jean-Michel Cousteau serves as "a voice of the ocean," educating students, conducting research, and producing films that promote awareness about the environment.

Jean-Michel Cousteau believes if you are in harmony with nature, you will appreciate the many connections we have to the earth. At a young age, he was taught to look beyond himself. The world is so vast, and so much can be learned from exploring it.

JEAN-MICHEL'S ADVICE:

My advice is to look at nature and try to understand how things work. Do you know how bees get sugar from flowers to make the honey that you enjoy, or how they carry pollen to fertilize other plants so that other forms of life can flourish? Everything's connected. We have to understand these connections. They're always there. Consider insects. Though many people don't like them, they contribute a very important role to our environment. So if you don't understand why certain animals or plants exist, discover their contribution to the whole before deciding to destroy them. Destroying one link may create a major catastrophe. The whole system may collapse.

I also want young people to know that there still is so much left to discover. Ocean life is one example. We know more about the hidden side of the moon than we do the ocean floor. There are new species being discovered all the time. Recently, a man I know just found five new species of fish! There are plants all over the Amazon that need to be studied to find out which ones can help us. Cures to illnesses are waiting to be found in these plants. We have an infinite number of opportunities still ahead of us. We haven't done and seen everything. It's all up to you, the future generation. You need to cultivate enthusiasm and keep it with you all of your lives. This is where true happiness can be found.

PETER LORD
Animator

born: 1953

 WHY PETER

Because Peter Lord is the artist who creates the clay models in animated films like *Chicken Run* and the popular and clever cartoon episodes of *Wallace & Gromit*.

Because as the cofounder of Aardman Animations, he creates each character slowly and with patience, until each move is just right.

Anything can happen and anything is possible if you have an open mind. Peter Lord believes in following your instincts and being ready to let them lead you on a different path. Embrace the surprises along the way, and life will be much more interesting.

PETER'S ADVICE:

Don't worry, something good will work out. I was never driven by a sense of time passing or needing to find a career. I think that was a great blessing. I know some people say if you want to be a ballet dancer, you get up every day at five A.M. and start dancing. That works, but in my case, what worked was being encouraged to believe I was good enough. If you believe that you are, something good will come your way. But don't be lazy. You can't sit around and do nothing. If you're hardworking, with an open mind and a positive personality, that's about 80 percent of it, in my opinion.

I absolutely think you should follow your instincts. That's such a cheap thing to say, but I think it's true. Set your sights high. For me, that wasn't about money. For me, it was believing that I was going to do what I loved doing no matter what. That's setting your sights very high.

CHRIS KLUG
Professional Snowboarder

born: 1972

 WHY CHRIS

Because national- and world-champ snowboarder Chris Klug says, "Bring on the speed." He's driven by the love of the sport. His positive attitude brings him home endless trophies and prize money.

Because after suffering from a condition called primary sclerosing cholangitis, Klug got a second chance on life after undergoing liver transplant surgery in 2000.

Because two years after the transplant, he competed at the 2002 Olympics in Park City and brought home the bronze medal.

Because he's committed to educating people about the importance of organ donation in saving lives.

Chris Klug's resolve never to give up has been tested on both a personal and a professional level. During his wait for the liver transplant surgery that saved his life, Klug was plenty scared. But he persevered. That stick-to-itiveness applies to all areas of his life, snowboard competition included.

CHRIS'S ADVICE:

My motto is simply "Never give up." Sometimes we're dealt a tough hand, but you have to make the best of it. Never give up, regardless of the situation or odds against you. In the quarterfinals of the Olympics, I was down by three-quarters of a second. I wanted a spot on that podium. I wanted the bronze medal. Wouldn't you know it, my boot breaks right before the run, so I grabbed duct tape and wrapped it up. Fourth place wasn't good enough. I was determined to bring the bronze medal home, and I did.

That same determination got me through three months of waiting for an organ match. I knew the odds. I knew that over 80,000 people in this country are on transplant waiting lists. I also knew that every day at least seventeen people die waiting for the right match. But until it was over, I was determined to fight and I did.

I also would advise young guys to follow your dream. I did with snowboarding, not because I thought there was a pot of gold waiting for me or that there was a future to be had in the sport, but because I loved to snowboard. I grew up dreaming about competing in the Olympics. Somehow, in the back of my mind, I just knew that snowboarding would get me there.

PERMISSIONS

Interviews were conducted with the following men:

Dave Barry

Glen Ballard

Robert Ballard

James Burke

James Cameron

Jean-Michel Cousteau

Hector Elizondo

Milton Glaser

Chris Klug

Chuck Leavell

Neil Leifer

Peter Lord

Martin Richards

Paul Orfalea

Kelly Slater

Danny Villanueva

INDEX